HOW TO WRITE YOUR FIRST NOVEL

WRITING YOUR FIRST BOOK FROM IDEA TO PUBLICATION

KATE KRAKE

INKWELL & ELM

CONTENTS

INTRODUCTION

Hello there, and welcome to the last day of your life.

Well, that sounded bleak.

Sorry.

Let me explain.

Welcome to the last day of your *old* life. In that life, you always wanted to write a novel. You were a "One Day Novelist"*, someone who said, "I would like to write a novel *one day*." You might have started writing a novel or ten, and you've probably quit writing a novel or ten. Or perhaps you haven't started at all, and you're still waiting for the right time, the right idea.

In that old life, you lived in a void state. You were an "aspiring writer." You probably know, deep down, that when it comes to writing, "aspiring" means nothing.

When I was growing up, there was an ad on television for Dreamworld, a family fun park on the Gold Coast, Australia. The jingle went: "Don't say one day, that day will never come!" My siblings and I would sing it to our parents whenever they put something off until "one day." I now say "one day" to my kids too.

"Can we get a kitten?"

"One day."

"Can we go ice skating?"

"One day."

"Can we go to Dreamworld?"

"One day."

"One day" is often a less confronting way of saying "No." You can get away with it because it's possible; these things *might* happen one day. But we all know there's a high probability they won't.

If you're sitting around saying that you'd like to write a novel "one day" then, unless you get up and *do* something about it, just like the Dreamworld jingle said, that day is never going to come.

So, forget "one day."

Today is the day you learn how to start writing your first novel, and today is the day you learn what you need to do to finish it. Today is the day you are no longer a One Day Novelist or an "aspiring writer." Today you step into your new life as an actual writer, someone who is writing a book and, in a few months, a writer who has finally written a book.

* I've borrowed the phrase "One Day Novelist" from Chis Baty of NaNoWriMo fame. There's more about NaNoWriMo in Chapter 6.

WHO AM I?

My name's Kate. I'm an author and former One Day Novelist. I write novels and short stories across the spectrum of fantasy, as well as poetry and nonfiction for authors and other creatives. I'm a proudly independent publisher, and I'm not a writing expert.

This book is not everything there is to know about writing novels. It's the basic version of how *I* write novels. Other writers may offer different versions, and you may go on to develop your own. This book suggests one pathway to novel completion, one I know from experience works. It's not a set of hard and fast rules.

WHAT'S IN THIS BOOK?

The book covers topics ranging from finding the right starting headspace all the way through to publication.

At the end, there's an appendix containing the details of books and other resources I mention throughout the text, as well as some extra info you might find helpful throughout your writing journey.

Mindset and Habits

In Chapter 1, we start with the most important thing you need to write a novel: a strong author mindset. This will include understanding why you want to write a novel and examining what has prevented you from doing it so far.

We then move on to writing habits. What does a sustainable writing habit look like? That will be different for every writer. We also talk about how you can create and maintain writing habits that fit your personality and life.

Ideas

In Chapter 2, we get into ideas on ideas. We look at where to find ideas, how to turn those ideas into stories, and which ideas are worth pursuing.

The Mechanics of Story

The next sections are all about the mechanics of storytelling, the nuts and bolts of putting a novel together.

Part 1 – Genre

Chapter 3 is all about how authors communicate stories to readers and how stories communicate their requirements to authors. This is genre. We look at why authors need to understand at least the most basic genre theory.

Part 2 - Character Arcs

In Chapter 4, we look at characters and character arcs—that is, who the people are in your book and how they change from start to end.

Part 3 – Narrative Structure

In Chapter 5, we explore narrative structure and how it relates to character development.

These three chapters will be the more intensive study areas of the book and the sections where you're most likely to come across potentially new concepts. Don't worry—this is a beginner's guide, and I'll be providing you with heaps of resources you can use to help the whole thing make sense. Remember, you don't need to know *everything* about writing a novel to write a good one.

Writing Process and Tools

In Chapter 6, we get into the drafting process and writing tools. This is where we talk about what you do when you sit down (or stand up) to write a novel. We talk about outlining a story before you write it versus making it up as you go along. This chapter will also explore some of the most widely used writing software and applications available to help you get the job done efficiently.

The Editing Process

In Chapter 7, we talk editing. Editing a novel could be a book in itself (and many books teach just that), so in this beginner's guide, I provide a quick run-through of my eleven-ish step process of editing a novel.

When Your Book Is Done

Chapter 8 is about what to do when you're finished. We talk about beta readers and critique partners, and a brief overview of publishing options. I debated whether to include this final phase content in a book designed to help you start writing your first book. Ultimately, I decided to include it because I think it's helpful to have at least an idea of where you want your novel to end up while you're in the beginning phases. Having a vision of your end goal helps stop any feeling that you're treading water, giving you something to work toward, even if it's something you might change your mind on later. And you're absolutely allowed to change your mind.

This book doesn't cover a vast amount on publishing, but again, I'll be directing you to resources to help you find out everything you need to know when you're ready to take this final step with a finished manuscript in your hand.

So…

Let's get you started on that manuscript.

A Note About AI…

When I wrote the first edition of this book in 2019, there was one reality about writing novels that I didn't fully consider. It was just a whisper back then, a speculation about a distant future. Five years later, that not-so-distant-future is a present reality and a juggernaut technology, so in this revision I have to consider AI writing tools.

I briefly discuss AI later in the book, but it's worthy of an opening remark. At the time of writing this book (early 2024), generative AI like ChatGPT can write novels that are good enough to sell in commercial markets. The tech can't spit out a complete novel on its own (yet) but it can generate substantial portions of prose which an author can engineer together into a workable narrative.

These engineered books might not be amazing works of literature, but they're good enough. Who knows what the next tech developments will do to those standards?! I've no doubt that this is just the beginning of what's possible in creating books with AI.

I accept this reality and so should you. This said, if you're reading this book, you're likely a human writer who wants to write your own stories. Just like me.

I support and celebrate the use of generative AI as a writing tool to help humans write human stories for other humans to read. I write about AI as a helping tool in Chapter 6.

With the ongoing development of this technology, all writers are being forced to question how this tool might disrupt our writing lives. There's little point in trying to compete with a segment of an industry that can churn out dozens (or more) of satisfactory novels in a day.

What we can do is embrace our human-ness. Write the stories that only we can write. Write the story that only you, a complicated human with a complicated life at this exact place in time and space, can write. And then connect with other complicated humans who want to listen to your ideas. If you choose to use AI tools to help with that task, then let that be an empowerment to your human creativity, not a replacement.

CHAPTER 1
MINDSET AND HABITS

When it comes to advice for authors, the mindset stuff is my favorite.

Why?

Because it applies to *all* authors.

Whether you've yet to write your first scene or you have a backlist thirty novels deep, a strong and positive author mindset is critical.

Every author needs a refresher in positive mindset at some stage, and understanding this when you're first starting helps you get through the struggles.

"You mean superstar billionaire authors sometimes feel this hopeless too?"

They sure do.

IN THIS CHAPTER...

- Why Start With Mindset?
- Identifying Your Motivations
- Drive
- Overcoming Your Obstacles

- How To Dedicate Yourself to Your Writing
- Ongoing Hurdles
- Sustainable Writing Habits

WHY START WITH MINDSET?

Writing a novel is different from anything else you've ever done, and each book you write will provide a different experience.

Writing a novel is intense. It's mentally draining; it's physically demanding; it's emotionally and even spiritually confronting. Writing a novel impacts your work life, your health, your family life, your social life. Writing a novel is hard work, and there will come times during the process where it feels too hard. If you're the kind of "One Day Novelist" with a few unfinished novels in your trunk, then you know this feeling all too well.

When it all feels impossible, it can feel like you're failing. It can feel like you, personally, are a failure.

When we're uncomfortable with something, our brains do everything to get us to somehow end that discomfort.

This is when we start second-guessing our writing. We feel out of our depth, confused, scared, worried about our talents or skills, and we fear judgment from others. Our brains try to start a new, seemingly much easier, and far less confusing story (also known as Shiny Object Syndrome), or worse, we're tempted to quit writing altogether.

By learning about author mindset before you launch into writing your novel, you prepare yourself for that feeling to happen so that *when* (not if) it hits, you're well prepared to recognize it as part of the writing process and say: "Hold on, Brain. I know what you're trying to do. Just trust me for a minute, and let's work through the hard stuff and get it done. I promise you'll feel great about it all when we're finished."

And *I* promise, there is no greater feeling than *finishing* your first novel, especially when you've been a One Day Novelist for such a long time.

This all sounds so simple.

Just ignore fear and carry on writing?

Essentially, yes.

But it's not easy. We all need help, strategies, tips, and tricks to get through. We need to fortify our mindsets.

How do we build these fortifications?

By identifying and understanding our motivations, recognizing and overcoming the obstacles of our false excuses, and setting ourselves up with smart writing habits that make it easier for us to push our fears out of the way.

IDENTIFYING YOUR MOTIVATIONS

I have always liked the accordion. There's something about the sound of it that I love, a romanticism that reminds me of my time traveling through Europe, exploring local folk music. Once or twice, I have thought about learning to play the accordion.

Why?

Because I like the sound, I like to watch people play it, and it gives me a nostalgic, whimsical feeling when I listen to it.

Is that enough to spend money on an instrument, or go to the trouble of finding one to borrow? Is that enough to dedicate so many hours to learning how to play it?

No.

I like the *idea* of the accordion, and I enjoy the work that other musicians do with it, but I'm not motivated to actually play one myself. I doubt I will ever be motivated.

Motivation is critical. Motivation drives action, and when we're talking about projects like novel writing, it's the thing that drives that action through all the hard stuff into completion.

To write a novel, you need to be motivated to do so.

I am motivated to write novels, stories, poems, self-help books like this one, articles, and essays. Why? Because I love making up stories, and I love helping others do the same. I love holding a book and saying, "I made this," and I love looking at my books on the shelf. I love building my life around creativity. I love hearing from readers that I've entertained, inspired, or educated them. That motivates me to get out of bed and put word after word for hours, to fight for the time to fit writing into everything else I want out of life. Writing makes me feel whole.

This is my why.

What's your why?

Take some time to think about your why, your deep motivations around your writing. You might like to journal your answers to the following questions:

- What motivates you in other areas of your life?
- Why do you want to write?
- Why do you want to write a novel?
- Why do you want to write this particular novel?
- How do you feel when you think about writing?
- How would you feel if you knew that you would never write a book?
- How do you feel when you are sitting down, writing?
- How do you feel when you've finished a writing session?
- How does it make you feel when you imagine your words in print?
- What do you hope for after you've finished?

You might find it useful to revisit these answers throughout your novel-writing process. Your answers may change as you learn more about what motivates you, what excites you, and what you discover you don't care about.

Why are we asking ourselves these questions? Particularly, why are we asking ourselves these questions at the beginning of the writing journey? Why know your why?

DRIVE

Knowing your motivations, the answers to these questions, will build your drive.

Remember that discomfort your brain is going to try to trick you into avoiding? Remember how we, as humans, are hardwired to quit when faced with a struggle? It's drive that gets us through these hard times and uncomfortable feelings.

Developing your writing drive will also help to provide focus and boost your wordy productivity; it is an excellent foundation on which to build your writing habit. We'll get to more on writing habits in the last section of this chapter.

Now you're getting an idea of why you want to write this novel. Now, we look at the flip side. Why not? Why haven't you written it yet? What has been standing in your way so far?

OVERCOMING YOUR OBSTACLES

In contrast to the motivational Whys, we have the Why Nots. Why Nots are the false excuses we *all* use, but they never seem false at the time. When we stop and take a closer look, we start to understand how we've been cheating ourselves out of our dreams and goals by creating obstacles out of excuses.

What has stopped you from writing your novel so far?

What makes you a One Day Novelist, an "aspiring" writer living in a null state?

Here are a few of the more common excuses of the One Day Novelist:

- I don't have time.
- I'm too tired.
- My kids are too young, too much work—I'll do it when they're older.
- I've got too much on my mind.
- I'll do it when work settles down.
- I'll start after we move house, or when… [insert any variable here].
- I don't know how to write.
- I'm not good enough.
- I don't know what to write about.

What have you been telling yourself about why you're yet to write your novel?

You might find it helpful to journal your answers.

Resistance

These excuses are all forms of Resistance.

In the writing world, the concept of Resistance was made famous by Steven Pressfield in his book, *The War of Art*.

> *On the field of the self stand a knight and a dragon.*
> *You are the knight. Resistance is the dragon.*

STEVEN PRESSFIELD

Resistance is the pressure of all those excuses listed above. Resistance is a feeling, a situation, a thought, a mindset that plagues *every* creator.

Don't feel you're good enough to try or to keep going? That's Resistance.

Can't find the time? Resistance.

Too tired? Resistance.

Just want to quickly clean the house before you start writing? Resistance.

Checking Instagram in the middle of your writing session? Resistance.

Deciding to wait until life is a little less rocky? Resistance.

Considering jumping to a seemingly easier project? Resistance.

Think writer's block is an actual condition? It's not, it's Resistance.

Overcoming Resistance

Get ready to hear the truth. Some people won't like it. You might think it's full of rubbish, that it might only apply to other people. Here goes…

You can dissolve every single excuse as to why you can't write *if* you want to write.

You have time. You have energy. You have focus. You have skill enough. You *can* write your novel now, but only if you genuinely want to move beyond everything that has been in your way.

So, how do we dissolve excuses? How do we overcome Resistance?

First, we have to recognize it and accept that Resistance is happening to us. Then, we think about why it's happening.

Why Do We Resist Things We Want?

There's a theory that unless we're talking about actual clinical situations like addiction and illness, all Resistance is born of fear.

That's certainly true in my life. Whenever Resistance has its claws in me in its varied forms, fear is at the core of the struggle.

What are you afraid of?

Not being a great writer?

Being ridiculed for being a writer?

Not getting published or not being successful?

Trying and not finishing? Or starting and not finishing yet another book?

Finding success and then not being able to sustain it?

I've listed these fears out of my own struggles with Resistance.

No one is a great writer when they start. We learn as we go. You can't expect to take up a pick and sculpt a block of marble into a statue without learning the craft. Writing is no different.

If you fear people ridiculing you for attempting to write, then keep it a secret. If people do poke fun at you for whatever reason, that's more to do with them and their fears than anything you can control, so why let it keep you from your dreams? Also, remove those people from your life as best you can.

Fearing not getting published? Work on your book until it's the absolute best you can do. Submit it to a publisher or agent and see what happens. Publish it yourself. Define your unique version of success and pursue it, adapting that definition as you move through life.

Are you scared of trying and not finishing? Then finish.

Whatever your fear, when it comes to writing, there's one act that will quell every one of these fears.

In Pressfield's words: "Do the work."

Dedicate yourself to the work, write despite fear, and Resistance will dissolve. Fear will likely always be there, but it's not in the driver's seat anymore.

Resistance takes a backseat when we find dedication. That's dedication to the work itself, the practice of the craft, and dedication to the time and energy it will take. We must dedicate ourselves to getting and staying organized, and we dedicate ourselves to daring to try and see it through to the end.

Here's what that looks like in detail…

HOW TO DEDICATE YOURSELF TO YOUR WRITING

Dedication to Being a Writer

Starting right now, you have to take yourself seriously as a writer.

Right now, dedicate yourself to being a writer with the same wholehearted enthusiasm you give to being a parent, a partner, an employee, or anything else important in your life. Being a writer needs to become a core part of who you are, even if that's just for the life of your novel writing project. Dedicate yourself to yourself and this aspiration you've been holding onto for so long.

If you don't have a 100 percent commitment to this, it's highly unlikely you will write your novel.

Dedication to Writing Practice

What does a dedication to writing practice look like? It's not pretty or glamourous. It's getting to the keyboard every day (or as much as your schedule allows) and writing words. One at a time. Some days, those words are going to stink. Other days, they'll be excellent. Some days they'll be fast, other days it will be slow going. The only thing these words need to be is consistent.

Forget making it good; just make it done. And don't even start thinking about perfection.

In the words of Voltaire, "The best is the enemy of the good." And in the words of my kid's school teacher, "Practice makes progress." When it comes to writing novels, progress is all there is.

. . .

Dedication to Time

One writing session isn't going to make you a writer. Nor will it earn you a finished novel. But lots of little writing sessions will do both. And that takes time.

Sure, some authors can and do write entire novels in a month. It's possible. It's not me, and unless you're an outlier, it's not going to be you. You don't need to be able to write a book a month. Nor do you need to be the author who sits for five years or more on the same book. With persistence and sustainable habits, writing a novel doesn't need to take years; a few months to a year is typically standard for most authors with good writing habits. For perspective, with young kids and a life just as busy as everyone else's, it usually takes me about six months of solid daily work to write a novel, less for a novella.

Commit to the time it's going to take. This is the time it takes to write, develop your habits, discover your process, and realize and prove to yourself that the things you thought were standing in your way are either insignificant or negotiable.

Dedication to Energy

Writing a novel is hard work. It's tiring. Writing fiction is one of the most mentally exhausting endeavors you can do. In the space of a single writing session, we can be making hundreds of decisions — decisions for our characters, plot directions, every word is one more decision. Decision fatigue is a real thing for everyone and writers even more so.

A tired mind is a fertile ground for Resistance to sneak in and spread its weeds.

To go the distance to write a novel, we need to think of sustainable energy.

How will you develop the staying power to show up to the next writing session, and the one after that? How will you gather the mental grit to recognize Resistance and shake off its thrall? It's all about energy management.

You know we're all working with the same amount of hours in a day, and we've all got busy lives. The difference between people who have the time and energy to write novels and those that don't is where and how energy is expended and conserved. That's energy management. With proper energy management, excuses relating to time and fatigue become non-existent, and when we do get tired, we're able to pull back before Resistance finds a way through the cracks.

What does energy management look like?

It's four things.

- Consistently good sleep.
- Consistently nutritious food and hydration.
- Consistent body movement.
- Consistent downtime for play and recreation.

This doesn't mean every day must be perfect in sleep, food, exercise, and play. I know better than to tell anyone with little kids that they should sleep more. It just means we need a general pattern of showing up to serve these spheres of life with as much balance as reality allows.

Dedication to Daring

If worries about not being good enough, or sharing your stories with others, are what's been holding you back, then dedicate yourself to daring.

Writing a novel is an enormous exercise in courage and vulnerability. It's a big deal! You're crafting an experience out of words, you're putting yourself and your life, opinions, and values into your work, and that can be extraordinarily confronting. Of course, we feel exposed and vulnerable. It's scary stuff! Don't worry, it should feel like this. That's what makes good stories. Unfortunately, this scary stuff stops a lot of people from even beginning their work.

There's always going to be something to make us scared. Why let that stop us from getting what we want?

Dare to write.

Dare to call yourself a writer.

Embrace that vulnerability.

Feel all the worry, acknowledge all the anxiousness, do the scary thing anyway.

Someone might not like your book. So what? Someone somewhere hates your all-time favorite novel. There are a handful of celebrated authors who I can't stand to read. That book you thought was so bad you couldn't even finish reading? Someone adores it. Every book attracts one and five-star ratings; that's a matter for readers and has nothing to do with the writing process.

You might be scared of people you know reading your work.

What if your parents read your book? Your husband, your kids, your boss, your old teacher, whoever?

If it's important enough for you, then don't tell anyone about your writing. Write it in secret and put a pen name on it. Or, remember that your story is your own and write it proudly. Others might have their opinions of it, and your mother might have a few mixed feelings about that sex scene you put in chapter four, but that's none of your business. Dare to own your work.

Do you fear failure? Good! Dare to face that.

What happens if you do fail? Great! Innovation is born in failure. Creativity can soar when original approaches fail, and getting out of your comfort zone, making mistakes, and finding new answers is where real growth happens.

Look at your list of excuses. How many of them are fear-based? How many of them do you dare to do anyway?

Daring, courage, and vulnerability are huge topics. For more, I suggest reading the work of social work professor Dr. Brene Brown, or at least listening to her TED Talk on the power of vulnerability. Details are in the appendix.

> Vulnerability is the birthplace of love, belonging, joy, courage, empathy, and creativity. It is the source of hope, empathy, accountability, and authenticity. If we want greater clarity in our purpose or deeper and more meaningful spiritual lives, vulnerability is the path.
>
> BRENÉ BROWN

ONGOING HURDLES

So far, we've talked about what can stop the aspiring writer from becoming an actual writer, and the mindsets and practices required to overcome these early hurdles.

But, the thing about false excuses and the Why Nots is that they don't stop once you start writing, and they don't stop when you've written a dozen books.

Resistance isn't a thing you beat once and for all. It's something you keep on beating as it shows up in all different guises, sometimes every day.

Resistance is a perpetual part of the creative life. It changes throughout your experiences in ways that are beyond the scope of this beginner's guide.

But don't let that put you off. If you get into the habit of working despite Resistance in this beginning phase of your writing journey, you'll have a far greater chance of recognizing and overcoming Resistance when it hits later on.

All of this talk about struggling and fear might seem

disheartening, and honestly, I'm not exactly painting the writing life in a very flattering way right now. But please don't be discouraged.

Understanding fear and Resistance is empowering. Knowing about Resistance, being able to name it, gives you complete control over it. Feel bad about your writing? "Oh, that's just Resistance." And then you keep going. Resistance goes away when you finish the project, and it's replaced by pride and satisfaction. Then you start a new project and begin the process all over again.

Sustainable writing habits help this all to happen.

HOW TO DEVELOP A SUSTAINABLE WRITING HABIT

A solid, sustainable writing habit, a reliable system of showing up to the page, is the way to ensure your novel gets written in the face of everything in your way.

Think about some other habits you currently have, such as watching TV after dinner, reading before bed, and making coffee in the morning. You do these things without thinking—they're just part of who you are. Imagine sitting down to your writing with just as little effort as you do to sit down to Netflix. Developing a writing habit is the process of ingraining the practice of writing into your daily life.

Like everything else about writing, developing a systematic writing habit is a process that takes time. You'll try different things. Some will work and some won't.

While different authors have different writing habits, there are a few commonalities to be aware of to help kick-start yours.

Find a Writing Time

First, find your time slot. Decide on a time you'll be able to maintain with some level of consistency. Early in the morning. Lunch break. Baby's nap. After dinner. When the kids are asleep. Whenever suits you.

Complete a time inventory. Take stock of everything you usually do in a week, as it's happening, and then look for patterns. Where is your time leaking away? How much TV are you watching? How much time do you spend cleaning your house? Commuting? Can you wake up earlier? Are you waiting for your kids to finish their sporting lessons? Can you combine any activities to save time? Can you cut anything or outsource?

It can also be helpful to stack your writing with another habit. Do you have a morning coffee ritual? Declare five minutes of writing will accompany that morning coffee. More on writing rituals next.

Find yourself a reasonable chunk of time. Thirty minutes is a good time and feasible for most of us, but novels can and do get written in ten minutes a day. Can you find thirty minutes one day, ten minutes on another day? It all counts.

The most important thing to remember about finding this writing time is consistency. You do not need to write every day. You can, and it's ideal, but it's not an option for everyone. You do need to write regularly. Once a week, once every few days, whatever works for your life in a way that you can reasonably trust to keep working. One day this week, another day next month, three days the week after that—that inconsistency will not shape a sustainable writing habit and will keep you a One Day Novelist forever.

Develop a Writing Ritual

Writing rituals are little habitual behaviors to help get you into the mindset for your writing sessions.

A writing ritual is a bit different from a writing habit, although your writing rituals are a part of your writing habit system. Writing rituals are something that you *do* as a part of your writing process that isn't actually writing.

I've had different writing rituals at different times in my life. Years ago, I was playing around with writing in the high fantasy genre, and at the start of each session, I would don a ring and a headscarf, and chime a small bell that had a certain inspirational relevance to the story. Once that bell sounded and I was wearing that regalia, it meant I was about to start writing that particular story. A bit silly, perhaps, but it worked. And it was fun.

These days I don't do anything so theatrical. My morning writing is ingrained into my other first-things-of-the-day routines—coffee and stretching—and later in the morning, my second writing session always starts with coffee and toast. Sure, I can write without coffee and toast and stretches (okay, maybe not without coffee), but I've imbued these actions with significance that connects them to my writing process.

Writing rituals are signals that engage our writing mind and say, "Let's get to work."

Other ideas for writing rituals can be, writing in the same space (if a dedicated writing space is feasible for you), wearing a particular piece of clothing, lighting a candle, listening to the same music either before the session or during, saying a prayer, rubbing a talisman, uttering an affirmation, and any number of things. Your writing ritual will be as unique to you as everything else in your writing life.

Set Small Writing Goals

Yes, you want to write a novel, maybe a series of novels, but that has to happen word by word, and that process is the everyday system you need to ingrain to reach that final lofty goal. In the beginning, while you're developing your writing habit system, focus on a small chunk of that overall goal. Start by just showing up. Open your computer. Write a single word. Easy. You're there, so you might as well write a bit more. Try aiming to write 50 or 100 words in each session. It's super easy to hit these incredibly small goals, and while they do result in your getting words on the page, the real goal you're achieving here is the act of showing up to write every day.

As you get used to writing regularly, focus on larger goals like 1000 words, a scene, or a chapter per session. For first drafting fiction, 1000 words a day is my favored amount. I can usually do it easily in an hour or ninety-minute session and it is a decent chunk of the story down. When I'm in editing mode, I measure my session goals in time (60 or 90 minutes) or chapters.

Know What You'll Be Writing in Advance

When we know what to expect before starting each writing session, we don't waste any time or mental energy planning and deciding. We show up, sit down, and start writing. This pre-work might come in the form of outlining your story before you begin writing (more on outlining in Chapter 6) or knowing only as far ahead as the beginning of the next session.

Many writers (myself included) find this is one of the many benefits of writing first thing in the morning, before the rest of life comes along to derail your thoughts. While I am going through my morning coffee and stretching routine, I am considering what I am about to work on. As soon as I open Scrivener, I know what to do and I set to work. Often I'll already know from the previous day's session, but it's good to have that ritual set the brain cogs in gear before I start work. Some writers ready themselves for their morning session the night before, relying on the subconscious mind to develop the ideas as they sleep.

· · ·

Maintaining Writing Habits

Writing habits, routines and practices will always get disturbed. Life brings interruptions, sometimes cataclysmic derailments. It happens to all of us. And then there are other impediments, usually Resistance-related.

There are seven main areas where our writing habits tend to find snags. These are related to both internal and external factors.

1. Crisis of Craft

Problem

You lack the skills or feel you lack the skills to write the way you dream your story should be. This sense of ineptitude paralyses your writing progress and derails your habit.

Solution

Practice. Write and write some more. Study writing craft books, listen to writing craft podcasts, read books you admire, and pick apart the sentences to see how their authors put them together.

2. Crisis of Confidence

Problem

You're not sure if your writing is any good. You feel like you're wasting your time. Your self-criticism is out of control. You think you'll never be the kind of writer you want to be. This lack of confidence feels so terrible that it's just easier to give it all up and quit writing.

. . .

Solution

Get some early feedback. Join a critique group or find a writing buddy. Remember why you wanted to write a book in the first place and focus on the process of writing, not the quality of the finished product. Become aware of your negative thought cycles and combat them with positive statements and affirmations, always focusing on what you love about the writer's life. Embrace the writer you truly are and start practicing acceptance of your unique writer's voice.

3. Life Gets in the Way

Problem

Life happens. Moving house, changing jobs, having kids, illness, renovations, vacations, Christmas, uh… pandemics. Life will throw anything and everything at us, and all of it has the potential to stop a writing habit in its tracks.

Solution

Understand the ebb and flow of habits. Your writing habit may need to change and adapt to different circumstances. Your thirty-minute session might need to be ten. Maybe you'll only write on weekends for a while. There might (will?) come a time when you'll have to put your writing on hiatus temporarily. If you have developed a sustainable habit and have taken the time to understand your processes, it's all the easier to jump back in when you get the chance. Practice self-care and look after your energy and health first.

4. Focus and Procrastination

Problem

You can't keep your mind on your work. The internet is everywhere, and oh, look at that hilarious cat meme… squirrel!

Solution

Distractions are never going away, so we need to learn to ignore them when necessary and indulge them appropriately. Work first, meme later. The same goes for email, social media, and anything else.

Arm yourself with some focus tools like Cold Turkey or Write or Die; put locks and time trackers on your devices. Get one of those mini safes for locking up your phone. Whatever it takes to at least temporarily release yourself from the strangle hold of distraction addiction.

Also, think about why you're getting distracted. Not as in "What is distracting me?" but why you're letting it steal your focus. Don't be surprised if you find Resistance lurking in your answer. It's easier and more fun to watch TikTok videos than it is to work on a novel. Of course your brain in going to choose that! Unfortunately, that part of your brain doesn't know what's actually good for it, so let that other, higher reasoning run the show. There's plenty of time for wacky video antics after your writing session.

5. Physical Energy Management

Problem

We all have times when we're too tired to write or are too tired to feel like writing.

Solution

Look after your body and energize and rest it properly. Remember food, movement, rest, and play.

6. Time Management

Problem

You feel you don't have time to write.

Solution

Evaluate where your time is being spent and honestly look for areas where you can borrow time. Most of us *always* have time to do anything we really *desire*. So, find that time!

Okay, so you might not have time to write 5000 words a day or even 1000, so write less. Take shorter writing sessions. A few words written in the stolen ten minutes while you're waiting for the bus is better than the zero words written while you're waiting to get more time. If it's hard for you to actually write in those stolen moments like kids sports or waiting rooms (it's hard for me), then use them to at least think about what you'll be doing in your next focused writing session, so you come to the page already primed for maximum wordage.

7. Uncertainty of Goals

Problem

You're feeling defeated and not seeing any payoff for your work. You're wondering if you want to be doing this whole writing thing anyway.

Solution

Go back to the beginning and find your why. Get into

yourself and search deep for the answers. Why do you want to write a book? Why haven't you done it so far?

And if it turns out that you absolutely, honestly and in no uncertain terms, do not want to write, quit. And do so with a light heart for having made the decision that's true to your desire. You can always come back if you change your mind.

CHAPTER SUMMARY

That brings us to the end of our discussion on mindset and habits. We've covered a lot of big ideas. How are you feeling?

In Summary…

- Choose to be a writer now. Choose to stop saying, "one day."
- Commit yourself 100 percent.
- Fear and excuses aren't going away—get to work despite it all.
- Start small to develop a habit.
- Look for strategies to adapt your writing to your life and your life to your writing.
- Things will always get in the way of your writing habit. Look for solutions to stop these interruptions from becoming total derailments.

Ready to write? What are you going to write about? Where do you get your ideas?

This is where the fun stuff starts.

CHAPTER 2
IDEAS

In this chapter, we're looking at the nature of ideas, and you'll also be deciding on your story. That's right, by the end of this chapter, you'll know what your novel will be about. If you already know what you want to write about, that's great! You'll be able to use the concepts here to fine-tune your thoughts and make sure your existing idea will work in the novel form.

IN THIS CHAPTER...

- What Is An Idea?
- Where To Get Ideas
- Capturing Ideas
- How To Turn A Raw Idea Into A Story Idea
- How To Find The Stories That Are Right For You
- How To Choose Which Idea To Pursue

THE NATURE OF IDEAS

What Is an Idea?

Ideas are intangible. Unlike stories, ideas are unstructured; they're more like emotions or senses. Ideas *become* stories, but ideas are *not* stories.

Ideas are cheap. They're everywhere, they're easy to come by, and most people, even non-writers, have them.

Some people, however, have *good* ideas, or they can work with an idea to make it a good one and then use that idea to make a good story.

Curios

When it comes to creative writing, ideas take many forms. They can be ideas for plots, or characters might leap into your head. Often I will observe something and think, "Oooh, that's interesting" and add it to my mental file. I call these Curios.

On the morning before I sat down to write this chapter, I encountered two Curios. I was with my daughter outside her school, waiting for her friends to arrive so they could all walk to class together. While little children played around me, and parents did their small talk, my eyes were on the tree branches overhead where I watched, transfixed as a raven dismembered a small bird. No one else seemed to notice, so I said nothing. The gore was one thing, but that I was watching it unfold in that innocent social situation was the particular Curio that snagged me. The second Curio of the morning was the texture and smell of butter. For some reason, I paid it careful attention while waiting for my toast, and it seemed like something I'd like to include in a story, somehow. Perhaps connected to murderous ravens? See how random, intangible, and fleeting ideas can be? By the way, that raven landed in my novel, *A Coven of Demons.*

My Curios lean toward the fantasy vibe—if you explore

my fiction, you'll see why. Your Curios might look different, but the process of keeping an eye out for interesting little bits that might work their way into stories is still the same.

When you're out and about, watching something, reading something, chatting, even dreaming, pay attention to details. What snags your attention? What excites you? Delights you? Repulses you? These are your Curios.

STEALING IDEAS

"What if someone steals my idea?"

This is a common worry with new and emerging writers. So people gather their ideas in secret, like greedy dragons hoarding gems—"I don't want anyone to steal my ideas!"

Don't worry. They won't. They can't. Even if someone does take an idea from you, the story they turn it into won't be anything like the story you turn it into. Stories contain billions of ideas, ideas contain billions of stories, and their possible combinations are infinite. In fact, it's good creative practice to give your ideas away freely, and in turn, steal ideas from others.

No, I'm not talking about outright copying stories. That's plagiarism, and it's bad.

Innovative ideas are familiar and easy to understand, but innovation also has a new edge. This edge itself is not new, but its novelty comes in the combination of ideas.

In *Steal Like an Artist*, Austin Kleon explores this very notion, delving into the ways our ideas are all connected to what others have made before us and celebrating the idea-stealing process.

Wait.

Doesn't stealing ideas make our work derivative? (Gasp! What a foul word!)

No.

When we gather these ideas, they filter through our own

experiences, our worldview, our preferences, our personalities. The ideas themselves and the way we combine them through our lenses are how we're able to create meaningful tales and genuine innovation. This is creativity.

So, to get creative ideas, we need to have lots of ideas and steal from everything and everyone.

If you think of creativity as "connecting the dots," we need to fill our minds with lots and lots of dots. These are the Curios I was talking about before, but they can also be bigger dots like writing processes, story formats, and anything any other writer has done that has captured your attention.

WHERE TO GET IDEAS

Here are a few places you can turn to find story ideas, the dots you'll need to "connect the dots" of creative thinking. All of these have given me stories or elements of stories in the past.

- Science or tech news—innovation overload!
- Random Wikipedia articles—addictive.
- Story structures from books and movies
- Trivia
- Obituaries
- Headstones
- Advertising
- Overheard conversation
- Music lyrics
- Random objects found in the street
- Random happenings witnessed in the street
- Novels (obviously) in form and content
- Picture books
- Things kids draw
- Things kids say
- Mythology and folklore

- Product packaging
- Movies
- TV
- Kids' TV
- Local news
- Documentaries
- People's daily lives
- Social media
- Mashups of multiple random story types (aka pastiche) (e.g., Cinderella meets a serial killer thriller)
- Formal writing prompts
- Music
- Visual art
- Shapes in the clouds
- Random social media accounts
- Textbooks
- Zoos and other tourist sites
- Public transport
- Tide pools
- Stock photography
- Generative AI tools
- …anywhere you go, anything you can look at, anything you can hear. Ideas are *everywhere*.

CAPTURING IDEAS

Many writers carry around notebooks; most of us carry around phones that do an excellent job of being notebooks. On a digital device, you can also record your ideas in audio (there are dozens of apps), or take photos.

Occasionally I'll write down the finer details of an early idea, but when I do, I find it stiffens it, lessens its power. I prefer to take a quick snapshot, or jot a few words, and then let these ideas simmer around in my brain for a while. Neil

Gaiman refers to this process as composting (he's a perpetual notebook carrier). Like gardening compost, this messy pile of ideas becomes fertile ground for stories to grow from, and every single bit of everything all breaks down together to create the same rich deliciousness of creativity. I find the ideas that are worth developing are the ones that will stick around, their heads bobbing up above the surface of the mind stew. Forgotten ideas probably weren't that strong in the first place, but they're all still in there, giving depth and flavor to everything else.

The process of capturing ideas is unique to every writer. As you move along your writing path, you'll develop your own system. There's more about note systems in Chapter 6 on processes and tools.

HOW DOES AN IDEA BECOME A STORY?

The writer's composting mind is a big pile of raw material.

Even if you've gathered the most amazing Curios, how do you turn these ideas into a story big enough to fit a novel?

Let's look at an example process…

For this quick study, I'm going to show you how to formulate a story from a raw idea using random Wikipedia articles as writing prompts.

I open up Wikipedia and click on the Random Article button.

Mo' Greens Please.

"*Mo' Greens Please* is the second album by American organist Freddie Roach recorded in 1963 and released on the Blue Note label. It was reissued on CD only in Japan, as a limited edition."

Okay. That's a fact. A cool fact. I love jazz, and Blue Note puts out the best of the best. But where's the idea? Where's the story? To find the story idea in the raw material, we need to go digging.

We ask questions and look for connections.

For example…

What does the title *Mo' Greens Please* mean?

Freddie Roach is quite a name… is it real? Did being called "Roach" give him any problems? What about a musician that is a roach? We could get a bit Kafkaesque on this one (see? Stolen ideas!).

CD reissued only in Japan? Could we imagine a die-hard jazz fan in Japan trying to find it? Why doesn't this person order it online?

Why not bring in more connections?

Click Random Article again.

Apostibes inota

It's a stub article about a moth. It provides details on coloring, length, and discovery.

There's an easy connection—moth and roach.

Maybe a moth and a cockroach are in a jazz band. Or an entomologist decides to take up jazz organ. Perhaps someone is in Japan for an entomological conference and somehow happens upon this rare jazz CD, and their life is forever changed.

See how it works? Examine the details. Ask questions. Connect answers and find stories.

But that only takes us so far. You might not have the slightest interest in writing a story about a jazz musician or a Japanese cockroach.

So… what kind of story are you interested in writing?

The most definitive answer to this comes through another question.

What kind of stories do you like to read?

HOW TO FIND THE STORIES THAT ARE RIGHT FOR YOU

What you like to read will, for the most part, be what you will be best at writing.

If you're not much of a reader, then I'm sorry, but forget being much of a writer.

Writers can be many things, but writers need to be readers. If you're a person who only cares about writing one novel, then maybe, but not without difficulty, you can get that book out without reading dozens upon dozens of novels beforehand. But if you're hoping to make a real go of this writing thing, maybe as your career, or a rewarding hobby, to get serious, you need to read a lot of books.

The kinds of stories we enjoy consuming as books, shows, movies, and games will be the sorts of stories we will most naturally create.

But what if I like to read everything?!

Me too.

For now, choose one. Sure, we have multigenre readers and multigenre writers (totally me), but start with a single focus and life will be a little easier.

How do your raw ideas connect to the stories you like to read? Consider the above roach/moth/jazz writing prompt. A romance reader will come up with a very different story than a fan of spy thrillers. As will an urban fantasy fan, a horror writer, a middle-grade author.

Now you try. Take your Curios or choose some prompts as I have above. Add in your reading preferences to shape the context.

What questions present themselves?

Who are the people in this world of your idea? What do they want? How are they troubled? How will they change? These four questions are the essence of all storytelling.

HOW TO CHOOSE WHICH IDEA TO PURSUE

Most writers will have heaps of different ideas, a lot of them decent. So how do we choose which one to pursue?

Even for fast writers, writing a novel takes a long time. You'll be spending months at least in this story world, so in addition to finding an idea you'll be suited to write, we have to find ideas that excite us.

I know the right stories for me are the ones I can't stop thinking about. For months, even years.

What excites you?

Think through your ideas and connections. Are there any that gave you a little thrill when you came up with them? An oooh! An *Aha!* moment? If you have multiple excitements, perhaps you can combine these ideas for a super-fascinating story concept.

The idea that excites you the most, the one that calls the loudest, that one is going to be your novel.

CHAPTER SUMMARY

How are those ideas shaping up for you?

There's a lot to unpack in the realm of ideas, and this is just the beginning of your journey into your creative workings. You'll learn more about the nature of ideas the more you work with them, so… get to writing!

In Summary…

- Ideas are cheap and everywhere. It's what you do with them that counts.
- The best inspirations are borrowed from others and combined with other ideas, to create fresh and original angles.
- The ideas you like to read about are likely to be the ideas you'll be best at writing about.
- The ideas that excite you are the ones you'll be best able to turn into a novel.
- Find a story within an idea by asking questions.

To add some depth and, more importantly, *meaning* to this idea, we now start to think about the mechanics of storytelling, starting with genre and tropes.

CHAPTER 3

THE MECHANICS OF STORY, PART 1:

GENRE

You'll often hear people talking about genre as if it's a dirty word. "Genre fiction? No, thank you! That's for hacks."

The truth is many people, authors included, don't understand what genre is and how critical it is for every single book ever written.

Genre theory is a massive academic field, one I first fell in love with during my first year of university. Through my postgraduate studies (most of them centered around media, communications, and cultural theory), genre theory remained my principal focus. Yes, I am a genre geek.

This chapter doesn't get that deep into academic genre theory but instead serves to explain what genre is, why it's critical, and why understanding genre will make writing your novel a heck of a lot easier and quicker. But, yes, there's a touch of academic theory in here because I can't help myself.

IN THIS CHAPTER...

- What Is A Genre?
- Know Your Tropes

- The Look And Feel Overlap System For Defining Genre
- The Reader Contract
- Genre And The Writing Process
- What's Your Best Genre?
- Learning Through Genre Immersion
- Avoiding Cliché

A note for authors intending to pursue independent publishing:

For indie authors, understanding genre is critical. Genre theory will not only tell you how to write your book but also show you how to cover your book, how to sell and market your book, and to whom.

WHAT IS GENRE?

Genre is not a box that stifles your creativity.

Genre is not an arbitrary system invented by book retailers so they know where to shelve books.

Genre is not shorthand for mass-market crap.

Genre is not static.

Genre is not limited.

Genre is not constricting.

Genre is dynamic and fluid.

Genre is a framework of communication.

Genre is a set of systems and conventions that allow a story to create meaning alongside categorically similar tales.

Humans categorize everything. We put things into frames so we can work out what they're all about and then we tell stories about those things. That's part of the experience of human consciousness.

As consumers, genre is how we decide what we like. In books, movies, games, TV, music, clothes, toys, furniture, art, genre is how we know what to expect. It prompts us into one section of the bookstore over another, one tab on Netflix over another, chasing a certain kind of experience.

As creators, genre gives us a step-by-step breakdown of what to write. Every novel falls into a genre and is written according to those conventions. Even the authors who seek to write some groundbreaking experimental think piece have to follow a set of protocols to create something that supposedly "defies conventions." The art-house rebel author still needs to make something that is *recognizable* as art-house rebel art to communicate to would-be readers what it is and why they should pick it up and give it a try. That communication is genre.

Now, many people balk at this concept.

"What? You're telling me to write a generic, formulaic story?"

Yes. And no.

Before we get into how to plan out a story, let's delve a little deeper into genre theory so you'll be able to figure out which genre you're working with, and how to understand it to develop characters and plot.

HOW TO IDENTIFY A GENRE

Know Your Tropes

Trope is another one of those "dirty words." We hear complaints like a story is "full of tropes" or that something "relies on tropes," meaning that the story was predictable and dull. But we can't avoid tropes; we need them. Tropes are the familiar, recognizable characteristics of a text. They are the building blocks of genre and stories.

All genres have tropes, and within that, all subgenres have their tropes. Recognize the tropes, and you can identify the genre.

Urban fantasy books typically take place in big cities and often feature fierce, sassy female protagonists. Shifter UF books often have a relationship between human and supernatural shifter. Supernatural bounty hunters, paranormal mysteries, and specialist investigators—these are all urban fantasy tropes.

In romance, we have the secret billionaire plots, the cantankerous love interest with a heart-of-gold. We have the sweet, reticent cowboys; we have the enemy-to-lovers relationship, the best friend who wants something more. Firefighters, nurses, strong corporate women, love triangles, reverse harems, happily ever after, and happy for now. All of them tropes.

In literary fiction, we recognize characters involved in inner turmoil or introspective searching. This can go further down into subgenre—relationship troubles, illness, mental illness, social injustices, minorities, self-awakening, and so many more. They all have their standard themes, and all of these themes are tropes.

Human vs. nature as a conflict is a trope familiar to horror. A cabin in the woods—that's a horror trope (and also the name of an excellent horror movie that played with tropes to an expert and thoroughly enjoyable degree). Home invasion, torture for fun, Lovecraftian monsters bigger than the universe—more horror tropes.

Individual power vs. power of a larger institution is a common conflict trope in thrillers. The wronged parent out for vigilante revenge, the rogue agent fighting the system, cliffhanger chapters, short scenes, choppy sentences, secret hideouts, damaged ex-military super-fighters, spies—all thriller tropes.

With so many facets and factors, tropes and genres can be slippery beasts, with dozens of subgenres, subtropes, nuances, and undefined, fluid boundaries.

Here's a way to wrangle that slipperiness into an easily understandable model.

THE LOOK AND FEEL OVERLAP: A SYSTEM FOR DEFINING GENRE

During my postgraduate adventures, I studied dozens of approaches to genre categorization and genre theory. One theory stood out above the rest; Rick Altman's Semantic/Syntactic approach to film genre.

Altman's theory is tied to cinema culture, particularly musicals. His original essay (referenced in the appendix) is mostly outdated and loaded with dense academic jargon, but the core of his model for understanding genre holds firm decades later.

Here I've reworked Altman's model for fiction authors (and readers) and repackaged the idea into a more easily digestible (i.e., less academic) form.

I call it the Look and Feel Overlap.

This system understands genre on two overlapping levels:

1. Look—the more physical elements of a text.

2. Feel—the more abstract aspects.

The Look

The Look contains all of the tangible elements within the genre. With books, this includes tropes like setting, character types, character situations like jobs or relationships, physical things in the story (clothing, guns, swords, whips, wands, parasols, horses, cars, makeup, computers, etc.). The Look also contains the book cover, the style of narrative voice, average chapter length, and the word count (different genres expect different length novels).

The Feel

The Feel elements are all of the intangible aspects of a book. This includes things like themes, emotional responses of the characters, plot elements. It also includes textual elements like pacing, metaphors, the wider cultural position of the book (minority groups, ethnicity, religion, etc.), and what kind of reader contract the book is seeking to fulfill (more on reader contracts soon).

Both sides work together. Feel elements give context and meaning to the Look, while the Look gives the Feel its location, appearance, and other physical references. Where these aspects overlap and dominate a story, we find its genre.

Let's look at an example using the western genre.

The Look of a western is classic. Tropes of cowboys and cowgirls, saloons, frontier towns, guns, horses, covered wagons, wilderness, plains, checkered shirts, boots, spurs, neckerchiefs, cowboy hats. Even modern western stories play with these "John Wayne" Looks. Contemporary western novels are typically short, usually involve at least one fight scene, and usually have a romantic subplot. You can see much of that just by looking at the covers on the westerns page of Amazon.

The Feel tropes of a western might include the relationship the honorable loner cowboy/girl/person has with their significant other or family, the sense of isolation in a lawless town, the spirit of the frontier, and the romance of opportunity juxtaposed with the harsh reality of the struggle.

If a character wears a cowboy hat and rides a horse, is that story automatically a western?

To use an example from cinema, in *Down in the Valley* (dir. David Jacobson, 2005), Edward Norton's character tries to be an old-fashioned cowboy despite living in modern-day San Fernando Valley. This film has numerous Looks of a western movie—Norton's costume is the biggest one—but the Feel elements, the story of the wannabe cowboy being a deluded man, deny *Down in the Valley* status as a western. The Feel markers of the plot, the drama, the tension, the romance overshadow the Look element of the cowboy costume, the horse, and other western factors.

While most texts have some overlap of genre markers, classification forms where the Look and Feel are the most dominant.

As such, *Down in the Valley* is a drama, even a suburban psychological drama to drill into subgenres, but it's not a western.

When Look and Feel Conflict

Unicorn Western is a fantasy series by Johnny B. Truant and Sean Platt. It's about a gunslinger and has all the trappings of a dark western, except the gunslinger rides a unicorn, and magic happens.

The Look elements are heavily western. The clothing, the settings, the character types, and heaps of other dominant tropes all shout western. The books rely heavily on western Feels too.

But then there's a unicorn. And magic.

The authors explain that this book could not have been marketed to fans of the western genre and instead pushed it to fantasy readers.

Why? It's got gunslingers, steeds, shootouts, saloons, and everything else that kind of western fan is looking for.

Because magic.

Magic, even just a teensy bit, plants a book firmly in the speculative genres and labels it as fantasy. Magic itself is the dominant marker and trumps the rest.

This trump card also applies to science fiction. You stick a piece of futuristic technology into your romance story, and you've just entered the hybrid genre of sci-fi romance. It doesn't matter that *The Time Traveler's Wife* by Audrey Niffenegger was mostly read by romance readers—it is still a science fiction novel.

THE READER CONTRACT

Honoring the Look/Feel Overlap is how authors fulfill the reader contract.

The Reader Contract is an arrangement between writer and reader that a book will meet certain expectations. Honor that contract, you get a five-star review. Break that contract, you're not going to sell that reader anything else ever again.

The genre makes the promise of expectations, and the subgenre makes the promise of how the book will fulfill those expectations.

Every genre makes its promises.

A horror writer forms a contract that promises the reader will be disturbed.

A thriller writer promises thrills.

A fantasy writer promises wonder.

A sci-fi writer promises social commentary alongside futuristic amazement.

A mystery writer promises a puzzle.

A romance writer promises a love story.

A crime writer promises a criminal case.

A literary fiction writer promises complex themes, struggles, and relationships written with elegant prose.

The subgenre further defines this promise with the specific clauses of its contract.

A sweet romance (sometimes called clean romance) writer promises a love story with no sex scenes and a happily ever after. An erotic romance writer promises a love story with lots of detailed steamy sex scenes.

A cyberpunk writer promises a certain attitude and action of character, and a plot reliant on technology.

A slasher horror story promises to disturb the reader with gore and intense tension. A fairytale horror story promises to disturb the reader with subtle unsettling elements and magical whimsy.

In hybrid genres, we get hybrid promises. *Alien*, a sci-fi horror, promises fear and futuristic amazement steeped in scientific concepts. *Firefly*, a sci-fi western, promises frontiers, honor, social commentary, and futuristic amazement—it's *Stagecoach* in space. Fantasy romance promises love and magical wonder.

Thinking about the Reader Contract helps us to drill down further what genre a story belongs to. For example, writers and readers alike often debate the difference between urban fantasy and paranormal romance. Here's the simple answer…

Yes, a paranormal romance is a type of urban fantasy. It has all the Looks and Feels—the metropolis, the sassy characters, the monsters. But, a paranormal romance has a romantic plot at the core of the story. Everything hinges on the love story and that love story is told with a predictable structure. General urban fantasy plots can be much broader. Sure, many UF books have a romantic thread, but that's not the main thing readers sign up for when choosing to read a UF book. It's not the core clause of the contract.

What is your story going to promise?

GENRE AND THE WRITING PROCESS

Now that you're an expert in genre theory, it's time to gather everything you know about your favorite genres and copy it to make your book.

Excuse me? You're asking me to regurgitate existing genre formulas to write my novel?

In a way…

Remember, as creators, genre gives us a step-by-step breakdown of what to write, but that doesn't mean we write boring old same-as-everything-else formulaic books. Just like The Ramones and The Sex Pistols did with punk rock, you're going to intentionally replicate the existing elements of your chosen genre, and make something truly excellent.

Length

Generally speaking, genre determines a novel's length. Most commercial genre novels (crime, romance, thriller, etc.) are about 60,000–70,000 words. If you're writing in fantasy, the subgenre determines the length—for example, most contemporary fantasies, including urban fantasy, fall into the 70K group, but an epic fantasy will be upwards of 100K.

The best way to determine how your genre should impact your length is to take a look through a bookstore and see what's selling.

More and more contemporary novels in multiple genres, particularly in the independent publishing world, are tending toward the 50-60K mark (anything less than 50K is technically a novella). Readers are as time-poor as everyone else, and with so much media vying for our attention, the demand for shorter reads is a definite reality right now. In recent years, super short romance novellas (around 10K words) are doing incredibly well in indie publishing, and that length trend is starting to seep into other genres. As usual, the ever-savvy romance authors are typically ahead of the publishing trends.

Writing a Unique Book with a Trope-Packed Genre Formula

You don't want to set out to write a romance novel and then go and regurgitate a bunch of Harlequin books. It's a fact of our present reality that generative AI can do just that. AI written commercial fiction books will saturate the market— and we likely won't be able to tell.

We're not machines. We want to write something with a human touch, an individual spark—that's the only way we'll ever compete with those mass-market AI books. But we do need to start from the same philosophy as the AIs. We need to study the core conventions of genre, but because we're not robots, we then need to model these standard forms into something unique that follows the same protocols but in our personal styles.

So, take up your idea from Chapter 2.

What genre is it?

What promises does it hold?

Is that going to work for you and the way you uniquely engage with stories?

WHAT'S YOUR BEST GENRE?

What genre works best in your creative brain? This is a bit different from the kinds of stories you like reading, but it is related.

It might be difficult to reach the answer to this if you've never written any fiction. But try nonetheless… when you think about writing fiction, what genre is at the forefront of your creative urge?

If you're a new writer, this concept might seem strange. Can't you just sit down and write any story in any genre by following the tropes and frameworks? Some writers might be able to do that.

I sometimes like to read psychological thrillers, and I know what to look for in a book description if I feel like reading something like that. I know, because of what those books need to contain (their genre frameworks), that I'd probably write a crappy one because my creative mind doesn't operate in those types of thrillers.

For some reason, beyond any human knowledge, whenever I write a story, it will contain speculative fiction elements. It's just a thing. I've tried to write serious literary fiction, quirky mysteries. I've written bad light romance novels and terrible contemporary women's fiction. These are all genres I enjoy reading, but when I sit down to make up a story, my brain is simply a speculative fiction writing machine. The last time I sat down to write a small-town contemporary woman's fiction story about the power of friendship, it ended up being about a demonic forest that drove hikers to suicide… and the power of friendship. It's just the way I'm wired.

If you're unsure of which genre you want to write in, try this experiment. Write a short story, as fast as you can—it doesn't need to be perfect or make a lot of sense. You're just playing with tropes, trying a Look and Feel on your idea like an outfit. Perhaps outline your thoughts in a few different genres to see how the story could play out differently. Where did your creativity fly the highest? Fancy yourself a romance writer, but can't not write about vampires? Then you might be knocking at the door of paranormal romance. Simply can't help but throw your characters into life-and-death peril at every turn? Perhaps you're a natural thriller writer.

LEARNING THROUGH GENRE IMMERSION

So, you've decided on your genre. You're going to write a crime novel, urban fantasy, space opera, or literary fiction, whatever.

Now, saturate yourself in it through total genre immersion. This is an idea I came across in Chris Fox's *Write to Market*. Chris talks about deciding to write a military science fiction saga and how, in the early stages, he immersed himself in the genre through film, TV and video games.

I didn't realize it until then, but this is precisely what I do, and I recommend you do the same.

Early in your ideation process, immerse yourself in your chosen genre. Read all of the current bestsellers and genre classics. Watch movies and TV series, play related video games if that's your thing. Read in the chosen format, novels, novellas, short stories.

Ask questions:

What do these texts all have in common?

How do they start? How do they end? How do their climaxes build? How do they resolve? Are they standalone novels or series? What kinds of characters appear over and over? What about the settings? Are they first or third person? How long are the chapters? Is there swearing, violence, or sex? What kinds of interesting ideas do they play with?

This is your genre formula, a guide to the length of your

book, how your story will look, feel, and what it will promise your reader.

AVOIDING CLICHÉ

It's unlikely that, if you've read this far, you're looking to regurgitate a bunch of plots and mash a slew of tropes together to come up with an unoriginal story.

But how do we work with tropes and not create unoriginal, clichéd stories?

What's the Difference Between a Trope and a Cliché?

A trope becomes a cliché when its recognizable qualities have become so familiar they have lost all impact. Instead of becoming part of a story, a cliché attracts a negative reaction, often of ridicule, and forces a reader straight out of the story. An example of this is the "orphaned farm boy is, in reality, The Chosen One" in the fantasy genre. Paradoxically, because a cliché has worked so many times before, we stop believing in it.

How to Use Tropes and Avoid Cliché

For starters, don't look to the tropes that have been done a thousand times before. Let's look past the Chosen One fantasy, or the geeky girl taking off her glasses in romance to become the super hot girl we've always known she could be if she just tried (*gag and eye-roll*). Instead look at the reasons these tropes became so popular. Everyone likes to think the small, dull person (i.e., ourselves) can evolve into something bigger, grander, more important, more heroic. What other situations can you devise that will fulfill that same wish without resorting to cliché?

We also avoid clichés by looking at tropes through new

angles or combining tropes to make unique yet still familiar ideas. How about a Cinderella-inspired serial killer police procedural story?

Or a haunted house story with a military edge?

The orphaned farm hand who's destined to be something besides The Chosen One (the arch villain, perhaps?). The newborn royal destined to be a peasant farmer and save the world that way?

The overarching genre in which you choose to develop your story will determine how one of these twisted trope stories would play out. For example, the twisted Cinderella killer would be very different as a horror story versus a domestic thriller story versus a dark comedy. The military haunted house would be different as a sci-fi story as opposed to a steampunk piece.

Take a look at your idea and all the tropes it *could* contain. Where can you twist those tropes? What new angles can you shape into your story? Can you add in a trope from a different genre to see how that might change things?

Now you're getting closer to true originality and genuine creativity.

CHAPTER SUMMARY

Genre theory is a massive field of study that won't ever wholly fit in such a short chapter or even a whole book.

For where you are now in your writing journey, all you need to know is the basics of what we've covered here.

In Summary...

- Genre communicates to both the writer and the reader.
- Every story belongs to a genre.
- Tropes are the building blocks of genre.
- The look and the feel of a story communicate the genre.
- Genre guides what you will write about.
- Clichés are overused tropes.
- The most original stories combine tropes in new ways.

Now, let's put those ideas and genre tropes into a formal framework and get to work to create characters and plot.

CHAPTER 4

THE MECHANICS OF STORY PART 2:

CHARACTER ARCS

Characters bring the raw elements of your idea to life. Without exaggeration, characters are the most important element in creating engaging stories.

You can have a great idea, and a decent plot, and know your genres and tropes backward, but if your characters fall flat, the whole package fails.

IN THIS CHAPTER...

- What Is A Character Arc?
- Creating Positive Character Arcs
- Genre and Character Arcs
- Character Function and Character Types
- Character Realism

WHAT IS A CHARACTER ARC?

A character arc is the process of change the character goes through from the start to the end of the story.

This change makes the plot happen.

There are three kinds of character arcs: the Positive Change Arc, the Flat Arc, and the Negative Change Arc.

A character starts somehow less; something in their past has brought them to this point. They then confront challenges that are appropriate to the genre. This person develops skills, learns things about themselves, tries, fails, learns again, tries different things. All the while, events, the plot, happen— sometimes plot happens because of what the character is doing, other times the character reacts to what happens to them. At the end of this process of trying, failing, acting, and reacting, the character grows into more. They're stronger, smarter, more proactive—this is a Positive Change Arc. If you're working with a more miserable tale, they end up defeated and in a worse position than where they started— this is a Negative Change Arc.

If the character does not change, this is a Flat Arc. This is seen most often in series with the same central character having a different adventure in each book (detective stories, for example). The central character doesn't change, but those around them do. We cover more on this in the upcoming section on heroes.

Whichever way the arc bends, the change in the character and the process of that change is what we're looking for.

CREATING POSITIVE CHARACTER ARCS

This is the most common character arc.

The Positive Change Arc starts with a character with various levels of personal discontent and denial. In the middle of the story, the character confronts these beliefs, usually because of external forces. In the end, the character has faced their demons and achieves a positive change.

In a Positive Change Arc, the character's discontent stems from a false truth they tell themselves, a deep, niggling splinter in their worldview. It's not a lie as such, because they truly believe this false belief is actual reality. It is the reason the character is resisting change as they go out to seek whatever it is they want. Out of this resistance, we get conflict, and out of conflict, we get the plot.

There's a reason this character has this false belief about themselves. This is the character's "ghost" or sometimes called "the wound." You've seen it in stories all the time—it's the aspect that haunts a character, mistakes in their past, things done to them, opportunities they missed out on, dark things that give rise to their present situation.

The more significant the wound, the bigger the false truth, the more struggle and higher stakes for the want, the better the plot.

In *Story Genius*, Lisa Cron urges authors to figure out what this lie is and the wound it comes from in high-def cinematic detail before writing a single word. This could be your approach. You might also like to see how your story emerges as you get to know your character through writing, and work in that past in later drafts.

What the character wants and what they need are rarely the same thing. Throughout the process of the plot, the character struggles to get what they want—and suffers a series of thwarts.

Along the way, they begin to understand the false stories they've been telling themselves and start to reexamine what they believe. This will result in them getting what they need, which is a lot more important than what they thought they wanted initially.

Change is key.

For deeper, richer plots, go through this whole process for

your minor characters as well and enmesh the various arcs throughout your plot.

GENRE AND CHARACTER ARCS

When putting together your story arc, you'll need to consider the genre you're working in, as different genres and subgenres have different types of character tropes and different arc tropes.

For example, in contemporary romance, we need both the characters to come through their respective arcs with a change for the better so that they can fall in love and get their HEA / HFN. Romance is always a Positive Change Arc.

In horror, you will need to consider what kind of ending you're going for—redemptive, hopeful, or hopeless damnation—and fit your character arc around that answer. Where your characters end up is where your story ends up.

The darker genres more easily allow Negative Change Arcs for obvious reasons. We also often see Negative Arcs in literary fiction.

Genres that work well with Flat Arcs are detective and police procedurals, serial adventures, and superhero stories.

CHARACTER FUNCTION AND CHARACTER TYPES

When we're talking the link between character arc and plot arc, we're mostly talking about the principal characters, those who get the most page time. There are three types of principal character, and how you design this character will influence their character arc.

The three types of principal character are:

1. The Main Character
2. The Hero

3. The Protagonist

These terms are often used interchangeably, but there are subtle differences.

The Main Character

The main character is the person who gets the most page or screen time. It's usually the character with the most point of view time, the eyes through which we see the story. A story can have multiple main characters for multiple sections. For example, *The Lord of the Rings, Song of Fire and Ice*—any narrative where the complete focus shifts to a different character for a decent time.

The Hero

The hero is the person who does the cool stuff, the admirable, the heroic things, but they don't change. The hero doesn't go through a character arc but prompts arcs in the characters around them. The hero solves the problems and takes action. These are the eternal characters like James Bond, Conan the Barbarian, Sherlock Holmes, or Miss Marple. In *The Hunger Games*, Katniss Everdeen is a hero character as she stays much the same throughout the books. Same too with Harry Potter. While everyone around him is evolving, Harry remains the same. Sure, he learns things and develops his skills, but at his core, he is the same person from start to end. It is possible to have stories without heroes.

The Protagonist

The protagonist takes the action that drives the story forward. This is the person who undergoes the most change. The entire plot of *Frozen* revolves around Elsa's character arc. Elsa is definitely the most interesting character (ice magic!) but her sister Anna is the main character. Anna also has her own arc, but Elsa's is the key to the story. Elsa is the protagonist. In *The Great Gatsby*, Jay Gatsby is the protagonist to Nick Caraway's main character.

While it's technically possible to write an entire book without thinking about these distinctions, knowing how each factor plays out structurally does help drive your story forward and deliver the right emotional impact at the right moments. It also helps to understand these distinctions if your story isn't working. If your characters aren't doing what you want them to, are you focusing on the wrong aspect of their personality? Giving them the wrong narrative role?

Understanding these distinctions also helps to work out the character relations and make for more dynamic interactions. How, for example, might a reluctant protagonist interact with an envious main character as they work through the same problem?

For more on an in depth discussion on these distinctions, listen to Season 13, Episode 1 of *Writing Excuses: Hero, Protagonist, Main Character.*

CHARACTER REALISM

You're getting an idea which direction to push your characters in, what you might force them to struggle against, and how you might get them to change.

Now, how might we think about making sure these characters are realistic? As writers developing characters, we're not just attempting to create something out of nothing; we're trying to create *someone* out of nothing.

Well-developed fictional characters have layers of personality on top of their basic arcs. To fully engage with a character, we, as readers, need to see a character's motivations and reactions that come in their arc, but we also need more external attributes.

Flaws

Think about your character's flaws. Do they have a critical flaw on which to hinge the character arc?

Beware of creating a token flaw.

"She was clumsy."

"He nitpicked everything."

"They overate."

The flaw needs to have a story function, a ghost, and impact the character's arc. Why does this person overeat?

How does food influence their decisions? Does their appetite get them into further trouble? What past wounds caused this person to be so critical of minor details? How else does this perfectionism show up? Is this person clumsy because of a physical situation or a psychological one? Maybe they're clumsy because they're chronically tired. So, why can't they sleep properly?

Diversity

In creating characters, think about diversity. We tend to populate our books with people like us and the people closest to us and forget what the real world is actually like. Consider writing about different cultures, ethnicities, gender identities, sexualities, and physicality, but beware of inserting diverse characters for the sake of token diversity. Like everything else in your book, character diversity needs to serve the story first. Do extensive research and consider using a sensitivity reader to make sure you've got all aspects of a culture correct and fair.

Trivial History

We all have a past that has a genuine impact on our present. We are all a product of our experiences, and your characters should be too. We touched briefly on ghosts from the past in character arcs, but now we create some broader strokes to color the character.

Think of everything that creates your personality—hopes, fears, tics, favorite things, pet peeves, sensitivities, passions, repulsions, great memories, etc. What's at the root of these things in your world? How, for example, are your pet peeves related to the town where you grew up? Why is that tic you have with your fingers related to your first school? Why do you wear that particular T-shirt to bed?

We don't need to include a full-blown history of our characters, just those things that are relevant to the story and help
to shape the arc, thereby driving the plot forward.

CHAPTER SUMMARY

Without realistic characters experiencing a strong character arc, a novel will never be great.

In Summary…

- A character arc is the journey of change the character goes through from the beginning to the end.
- The character's arc is rooted in their past.
- There are different types of characters that function differently within different stories.
- Realistic characters are essential for well-rounded stories.

How do the character arc and the plot intersect? This question takes us into the third part on the mechanics of story as we start to explore the basics of narrative structure.

CHAPTER 5
THE MECHANICS OF STORY
PART 3
NARRATIVE STRUCTURE

This chapter is about the shape of stories. We look at how to develop the character arc and plot with a beginning, a middle, and an end.

Our minds are ingrained with stories and story structure. For our whole human history, we have been telling stories in the same shapes. We know it, and when we start to take a closer look at it and break down the components of story structure, it seems obvious. We can study it until we're cross-eyed. We can recite Aristotle's *Poetics* by heart. We can recognize the archetypal feminist journey of *The Virgin's Promise*, or know any other structure theory inside out, and yet when we sit down to actually do it, even writers who have written dozens of novels can have a hard time working out what best goes where. Narrative structure is intuitive, but that still doesn't mean we're born knowing how to put a complicated story down on paper in perfect order. Don't let this put you off. All that's needed to know for the beginning novelist is the basics, the foundation of story structure, and where to look for the next levels of study when you're ready to advance.

Story structure is one core with countless variations.

That's why there are so many methods for understanding essentially the one thing.

We can't go through all of those methods and variations here; no single book could. There's too much information, too many possibilities. Here we'll look at basic story and a few concepts for tightening the narrative in smaller, easily digestible chunks.

IN THIS CHAPTER...

- The Three Act Structure
- Scene Structure
- Scene Pacing
- Learning And Writing At The Same Time

THE THREE-ACT STRUCTURE

In the Western culture, stories mostly operate on a core three act structure.

1. Beginning.
2. Middle.
3. End.

Theorists have broken this down into different variations. A couple of examples:

Four-act structure divides the middle with a story-turning event, usually a moment of decisive change for the main character. It's still three acts.

A seven-act structure adds formal crisis points and recovery scenes to the core three acts.

There are many others. To start writing a novel, and finish it, all you need is a grasp of the three-act story structure and how it connects to a character arc. Once you've got that, you can explore other narrative nuances at will.

1. Beginning

The beginning of the story is the first 25% of the book. Roughly.

Say you're writing a typical genre novel, about 70,000 words. For the first 17,500 or so, you'll be following a particular series of events as you set up the story. This is where your character encounters the problem that will set their character arc in motion. The character is reactive to stuff happening to them. In a murder mystery, you'll meet the detective, or sometimes the person who'll hire the detective, and find the body. In a romance, you'll meet the single person/people and then have the would-be couple meet one another.

This initial set-up typically breaks down with a hook, inciting incident, and a call to action.

The Hook

The hook is the thing that gets your reader into the book. The hook, the opening bang, is the little promise to the reader that you're going to give them something that's worth their time.

A narrative hook is attractive, but how you form that attraction depends on your genre. In the first *Harry Potter* book, the hook happens with the slow murmurings of magical activity throughout London that occur in the opening pages. In my supernatural mystery, *A Maze of Murder*, the hook is the introduction to Belinda Drake as an unskilled witch who has run from something in her past and wound up working in a bookshop in a quaint mountain village, a complexity that's condensed into a few pages before the inciting incident.

The Inciting Incident

There is one point in your story beginning that truly kicks things off. This is the inciting incident. Many writers will make their inciting incident and the hook the same thing, but a little "getting to know you" preamble hook is perfectly fine before the inciting incident. It usually happens before the 12% point.

The inciting incident in a murder tale is finding the body. In a romance, it's the moment the couple meets (the "meet cute"). Harry Potter learns he's a wizard. The inciting incident is the point from which the rest of the story flows.

After the inciting incident, the characters will usually mill around with it for a while. This incident has forever altered their world. They have been called to adventure, chosen for a mission, met certain ally characters, and asked to make a choice. This typically takes us to 25%.

By the 25% mark of the story, key events need to have occurred to ensure they accept that call to action.

. . .

2. The Middle

Once the character has made their choice and accepted the call, they're now officially off on their quest (very literal for those writing quest fantasy). This is the start of the story middle. The Hobbits have taken their first steps out of Hobbiton. Harry Potter is standing on Platform 9¾ for the first time. Your sleuth has taken on the case. The romantic lead has decided that maybe they should pay attention to this new person who has just fallen into their life (whether that's good or bad attention depends on the tropes of your chosen romantic subgenre).

The middle is where things get increasingly complicated. Essentially, it is a process of try, fail, try something new. You often see this referred to as "progressive complications" in narrative theory guides.

For the first half of the middle, your character will be reacting to external situations as they struggle to get what they want. Everything will be in their way, from the antagonist's actions to their own faults and the false truths they tell themselves about what they want. Every progressive complication changes the character in some varying amount.

The middle takes up 50% of the story as a whole.

At the 50% mark of the story (37,500 words for a standard 70K), the characters encounter something big. This is a game-changing event that, in some way, alters who they are. It's not the climax of the story, but it's the peak of their character arc, the point where significant change happens.

From this point on, the character knows new things or has new skills. They understand what they're doing and what they're after (more or less, they'll still have conflicts after all) and have decided how they're going to get it. This is the point where your character shifts from being reactive to being active.

As the story now moves towards the 75% mark, or the start of the third act, the stakes continue to increase. The character is fully invested and has to see things through. They have changed forever, but they're still not the person you're setting them up to be at the very end.

3. The End

At the 75% mark, we get the climax. This is the big fight scene, the Big Boss monster, the final tipping point where the couple will either get together or fail forever in the face of the grand romantic gesture. Everything is on the line, everything hangs in the balance.

Over the final 25%, we move through the end. The climax plays out, and the chips have fallen. Now, how does the world move on from here? At this point, the narrative stops putting out questions and starts to make sure everything gets answered and all the problems are solved. The character understands what they need, perhaps has healed their wounds (or at least understood themselves better), and their character arc is settling them into a whole new person.

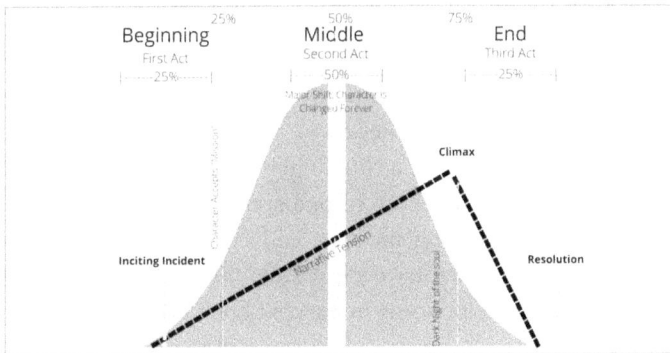

That's the bird's-eye view of a basic three-act structure. Now we move on to the smaller components of the story and look at scenes. But here's a sneak peek… we write scenes in the same form.

SCENE STRUCTURE

The same three-act macro view of the whole story also applies to the structure of each scene.

Like the whole book, every scene starts with a hook and has an inciting incident (remember, these can be the same if you choose).

Then, a problem happens to prompt a change, and complication ensues.

We get a crisis where the character must make a choice. Action happens, and complications increase. The character is changed in some way and moves into a resolution that sets up the next scene. Repeat.

This is the basis of the Five Commandments Of Storytelling from Shawn Coyne's *The Story Grid*.

J. Thorn, author and Story Grid editor, condenses this model into the Three Cs:

Conflict—something happens to move a character into action.

Choice—the character must choose how to act.

Consequence—the results of the character's action.

See? It's the same beginning, middle, and end structure that the whole story operates on.

Here's a tip: to create a cliffhanger scene, end on the choice and move the consequence of one scene to the beginning of the next as an inciting incident and conflict. Put that next scene in the next chapter or, if it suits the reader promise of your genre, finish the scene in the next book in the series.

SCENE PACING

Turning The Scene

When you're putting together scenes, make sure each scene turns.

What does turning the scene mean?

Have each scene start on one condition, and turn it around by the end of that scene. Start the scene as hopeful and end hopeless. Start as miserable, end in joy. Start in clarity, end in confusion. Start in death, end in life. This keeps the novel's pacing moving along, enticing the reader to keep turning those pages.

Yes, But... No, And....

I first came across "Yes, But... No, And..." through the *Writing Excuses* podcast. It's a succinct way of thinking about progressive complications. Structuring your action with Yes, But... No, And... this provides compelling pacing, always moving the story forward.

Here's how it works:

Your character is trying to achieve something.

YES, they achieve it...

BUT, something negative happens as a result.

or

NO, they fail...

AND, something worse happens as a result.

For example:

YES, the hero escapes the plane wreck in the jungle.

BUT, they then fall off a cliff.

YES, a jutting log saves their fall.

BUT, now there's a snake winding along the log coming right for them.

YES, they kill the snake.

BUT, now they're falling into white rapids.

Alternatively:

NO, the hero cannot escape the plane wreck in the jungle.

AND, there's a hundred snakes coming after them.

NO, they cannot escape the snakes.

AND, now the Arch Villain is there, laughing at their inevitable demise.

Combine sequences of Yes, But… together with No, And… and you've got yourself an action-packed page-turner of a novel.

LEARNING AND WRITING AT THE SAME TIME

This is where I hand you a stack of books on story structure that will guide you through the finer details. You'll find that stack in the appendix. I hope that after this brief introduction to formal narrative structure—which is enough to get you to write a novel, I promise—you will take a deep dive into these texts.

If you do get into the nitty-gritty of studying narrative, nothing is forcing you into one model over another, or even one formal model at all. You might choose to follow a more traditional level of detail like The Hero's Journey, or something more abstract and contemporary, like *The Virgin's Promise*. You could go through *Save The Cat* scene by scene. You might write your novel off the top of your head and then go back through and edit it strictly according to *The Story Grid*.

You might pick and choose from all of them.

You might read *The Story Grid* and forever change the way you think about turning scenes, but stick with Libbie Hawker's recommendations on how to get your side characters helping the protagonist, structuring those scenes to *The Three Story Method*.

Or, you might simply write your story, beginning, middle,

and end however it occurs to you and never even think about these books.

Studying these methods is not mandatory, but it does help. You can write a novel without knowing it all, but you will write a *better* novel once you start to recognize these narrative patterns. That doesn't all have to happen in your first book or even your second.

Warning!

Many new writers get caught at this point, trying to learn all the ins and outs of narrative theory before writing their novel.

Don't be that writer.

The best way to learn this stuff is to write and study at the same time. It's your application of this theory that will really cement it in your mind. If you learn something new and want to try it after you've finished your novel, then go back and apply what you've learned in revision. Or write a new book.

An aspiring writer who waits until they've learned every-thing before they start writing, will forever remain an aspiring writer and will never write their first novel.

CHAPTER SUMMARY

These last three chapters have been a lot to take in, especially when you might not have a clear idea of your story or where it's going to end up. That's okay. It will make deeper sense as you continue to learn and write.

In Summary...

- We understand stories through frameworks.
- There are countless frameworks on which to develop a story.
- Mostly, stories have three acts: 1. Beginning, 25% of total word count. 2. Middle 50%. 3. End 25%.
- Stories start with an inciting incident, develop progressive complications, climax, and resolve.
- Progressive complications build tension and create pace.
- Scene structure works the same as the whole story macrostructure.
- Story structure is something you can never stop learning. Different approaches can be combined.
- Learn through writing and while writing.

How you approach working your ideas and characters into a narrative framework will be largely dependent on your writing process, whether you're a planner or a discovery writer, a fast drafter, or a cycle drafter. That's what we're going in the next chapter.

CHAPTER 6
WRITING PROCESSES AND TOOLS

In this section, we're going to look at ways to sit down and write your novel.

Every writer has their unique process, and what works for one won't work for another. Most writers will see their process evolve, changing over time, even from book to book.

When you're beginning your writing journey, the important thing is to pick a starting process. Decide you're going to outline, or you're going to discovery write, fast draft or cycle draft, and start with that process. You might find that as you go along, you'll try one method and then switch to another and realize you're better at that. The same goes for writing tools. Start with what you have and see what works.

The point is to start.

IN THIS CHAPTER...

- Pantsing Vs. Plotting (Discovery Writing Vs. Outlining)
- Writing The First Draft (Fast Drafting, Cycle Drafting, Editing as Your Write)
- Writing Tools

PANTSING VS. PLOTTING (DISCOVERY WRITING VS. OUTLINING)

If you've listened in on writer's circles, you might have come up against the terms plotting and pantsing, also known as outlining and discovery writing, architecture writing or plot gardening. Whatever you call it, it's a dichotomy of pre-planning a plot in notes vs. winging it in prose. Often writers position themselves firmly in one group or another, but as we'll see, this isn't an accurate distinction.

Pantsing (Discovery Writing)

Pantsing refers to the phrase "writing by the seat of your pants." These are the writers who wing it all, making it up as they write. There's no pre-planning beyond any mental notes, and even this is optional. You might also hear this referred to as writing into the dark, or organic writing.

Discovery writing typically only works well when you have the elements of story embedded into your brain. Not every aspect of narrative structure we've encountered in the previous chapter will come out in your first draft. Much of it will need to be inserted and shaped during the editing phases. Still, the core of it—the beginning, the inciting incident, the middle build of conflict cycles, the climaxes, and resolutions—should be roughly in place in the first draft.

Plotting (Planning or Outlining)

Plotters are writers who formally work out what their story is before they start writing the actual prose. Some planners do this with a heavily detailed outline, others do it with a general guidepost system of plot, genre, characters, inciting incident, and major story events.

. . .

Why Pantsing Vs Plotting is Irrelevant

We don't need to polarize these practices. Discovery writing and outlining are two ends of a complicated spectrum.

A draft written with no pre-planning is a highly detailed outline, and an outline of any kind is discovery written.

Discovery Outlining – The Best of Both Worlds

Many writers swing around in the middle of this continuum. It's a process of pre-planning the book's major plot points, the essential shifting points such as the inciting incident, the critical character arc moments, and what happens in the end. Once you have these in place, you're free to fly wildly between each one, inventing the journey as it happens even though you know the destination.

You don't need to be one end of the spectrum or the other for everything you write. After making a giant mess discovery writing my first novel, I used to believe I was a dedicated outliner, with some moments of discovery writing. I typically started with a signposted outline. I'd brainstorm a lot of detail by hand in notebooks and then turn to Scrivener to do a detailed plan for the first 25%, scene by scene. Approaching the 50% shift, I'd develop less detail but still have some idea of the main story beats. The ending would be clear in my mind, but the events between the beats at 50% and 75% and then 100% were typically discovery written. I've written eleven novels with the general system described above. But then my most recent novel (*Night Shift At The Shadow Bay Hotel*), I let evolve organically from the first word. At around 80%, I went back to the beginning of the draft and re-structured it into something more cohesive than the tangle of random events it began with, and then once again winged it to the end.

I am not sure what prompted me to write that novel into

the dark, but I did and I've never had so much fun writing a novel, and plan to do it with my next story too. I expect one day I'll pre-plan a novel again and continue swinging back and forth as my creative drive takes me.

Should You Plot or Pants Your First Novel?

In the first edition of this book, I encouraged emerging authors to outline their first book. It's a valid strategy for keeping on track when, not if, the writing gets tricky.

However, see above about me discovering I love discovery writing.

I believe the only way I was able to successfully discovery write that novel because after so many years, story structure is ingrained in my brain.

Many writers can and do very well pantsing their first novels. The only way you will know if you are one of those writers, is to try.

If outlining turns you off, then write your novel into the dark, by the seat of your pants. If it's too hard, too messy, has too many problems, then stop. Retroactively outline what you've written, and outline the rest. Start writing again and see what happens.

Just keep writing.

A Note on Pre-Planning World-Building and Research

World-building refers to the artificial world you create for your characters to inhabit. The phrase world-building is typically synonymous with fantasy authors working in imagined locales, but every work of fiction, even those with contemporary real-life settings, requires some on-page world-building.

World-building around real places you know well can easily be done on the fly as you write. In everything else—historical settings, foreign settings, entirely fictional settings—

world-building will require some element of pre-planning and research.

World-building is a slippery trap for many new writers. I've known would-be writers who've spent years in the world-building phase before getting into the actual writing, some who have never started writing. It's just not necessary.

Research and pre-plan only as much as you need for your story to be credible, and write and research simultaneously. No, don't research during your dedicated writing time. Just make a note of anything you need to find out as you're writing and do the research at a different time. Come back and fill in the gaps at your next writing session or during an early revision phase.

Now…

You've got your outline, or you're braving writing into the dark. It's time to start writing.

Buckle up. You're about to become a real writer and start that first draft.

WRITING THE FIRST DRAFT

You're ready to write. You sit down at a fresh, clean page, position your fingers over the keyboard. The story landscape stretches out before you, full of adventure, the high points you already know and can't wait to get into, plus the giddy thrill of what you're about to discover along the way as your story takes on a life of its own. Your characters are ready to breathe. You're ready to write.

You type your first sentence, your opening paragraphs. Your chest tightens, and your stomach drops. Dread creeps in.

You've written a clunky pile of crap. How could you be such an awful writer? What even are words anymore? You're tempted to rewrite it. Or maybe even quit altogether?

What do you do next?

In this section we'll go over how to get words onto the page without that dread feeling derailing your words, and how to welcome those awkward sentences that we all write.

Fast Drafting

Fast drafting is when you write the whole first draft of your novel, start to finish, as fast as you can. Fast drafting is also known as the Vomit draft (eew!), the Dump draft (still eew!), the Alpha (my term) or Zero draft. Anne Lamott famously calls it the Shitty First Draft. Whatever you call it, the principle is the same—write first, think later. It's incredibly liberating.

Fast drafting means no editing, not even for typos. You can write in fully detailed scenes. You can write in scenes that just contain the dialogue (more on Skeleton Drafting later in this chapter). If you encounter something you need to research, make a note, keep writing, and do the research later. Come back and fill in the details in your next writing session or during the editing phase. I even do this for character names, using holders like FMCNAME and BADGUYNAME through my Alpha drafts.

What? You can't even fix a typo?

Nope, not in my rules. Others say it's fine to fix typos, I say "Why bother?"

What is this madness?!

Fast drafting was a life-changing process for me. Fast drafting made me a writer. I first learned the power of fast drafting in NaNoWriMo 2008 when I wrote my first novel (more on NaNoWriMo later in this chapter). It was rubbish, but that's okay—I wrote it and got it done. If it wasn't for learning the power of fast drafting, I would never have written a second novel, a third, or even this book.

• • •

Why Fast Drafting Works

Writing a novel requires two different and opposing parts of your brain; the creative free, experimental and daring, playful part, and the editing analytical, serious part. When you're in the first draft mode, figuring out your story and letting the characters and their world flow out of your mind, you need the creative freedom part—yes, even if you've pre-planned your book.

You need to let go of your inhibitions and ideas of right and wrong. You need to permit yourself to be a crappy writer because, in the beginning, we all are.

You need to get into a flow state where you don't even notice your fingers moving across the keyboard as the characters really do feel like they're coming to life. Fast drafting allows all of this.

Every time you fix a typo or edit in any other way, you're taking your brain out of this creative wonder flow mode and pulling it back into the rigid world of rules and analysis. This is Editing Mode. Stories don't get written in this part of the brain. What's more, this is the same part of the brain that will tell you that everything you do is rubbish, and you should just quit now and move on with your life. Do you want that brain in charge before you even finish your first draft? Since you're reading this book, I would say no, you don't.

So, switch off your editing brain.

Keep writing, as fast as you can before your inner critic gets a chance to catch up with what you're doing. If you have an idea for something that occurs earlier in the story, make a note, and then keep writing where you're up to as if that had already occurred. When you get to the editing phase, you can go back and add in all the extra bits. This includes adding in things you need to cross-reference or research—make a note, and then add it in later.

Write and write and hold nothing back.

If the Editor does pop in as you're writing (and it will), tell it politely, "Okay, I'll listen to you when it's your turn to speak. For now, Creative Freedom Brain has the floor, so please, get out of the way. You'll have your turn to shine, I promise." And then carry on making a beautiful mess.

NaNoWriMo

A book that promotes fast drafting a novel must talk about NaNoWriMo. NaNoWriMo, or National Novel Writing Month, is an online writing event held every November, where thousands of authors at all stages of the craft come together to write a 50,000 word novel in 30 days.

What? Seriously? That's nuts.

Yes, it is.

It's also wonderful.

There's nothing quite like getting up on November 1 (and many have the annual tradition of staying up until midnight —until I had kids, I was one of them), and knowing that you're one in a massive team of novelists, all working alone but all working together to do one crazy thing simply for the sake of creativity.

On November 1, you start writing. It's 1667 words a day. It's fast, and it's messy. It forces any false idea of perfection to take a hike and sends your inner editor flying to the backseat of your high-velocity novel writing speed machine.

NaNoWriMo provides structure, encouragement, community, instruction, and a goal. Writers from all types of lives amaze themselves with just what they are capable of writing when simply permitted to write fast and write badly. Sure, some authors edit their NaNo novels as they go. To me, that's contrary to the spirit of the event, but whatever gets you to the finishing line is just fine.

You don't "win" anything besides the satisfaction of writing a ton of fiction really fast. When you do it, you'll understand that no prize money or trophy could ever feel better. I've done it thirteen times over sixteen years, and even though I will never publish or even revise most of those stories, I have the event to thank for making me a writer.

Skeleton Drafting

Skeleton drafting is a fast drafting process in which you write down the bare-bones version of your story. It's not outlining, as there's a lot more depth and detail, but it's still not fully detailed pages. An example of a skeleton draft would be something like, "She opens the door and goes inside, feeling nervous." In the revision pass, you'd change that to something like, "Cold fear gripped her throat while her hand pressed against the chill chrome door handle." I've also heard of authors writing a skeleton draft using only dialogue and basic direction, rather like a script.

By skeleton drafting, you're getting the story out fast, including all of your scene details, and saving your max creative juices for the big picture stuff instead of thinking of delicate ways to construct your sentences. That part is for revision.

In my experience, fast drafting is the only thing that works. But that's just me. I know some authors who speak of the fast drafting process with similar reverence, but some authors hate it and would rather not write at all than even consider doing it. There's room for both in this world.

Cycle Drafting

For those who think fast drafting might be something akin to torture, you might consider cycle drafting.

Cycle drafting is a method of editing as you go, but doing it in such a way that you're fast drafting in sections and then editing those sections.

You write a certain amount, say 500 words or a page, and then go back and edit them before moving onto the next part of the story.

The proponents of this method claim that you end up with a cleaner first draft. However, I argue that what you end up with isn't a first draft at all but rather a polished draft that has gone through its revision processes in stages.

Pros and Cons of Fast vs. Cycle Drafting

Both fast drafting and cycle drafting result in finished stories, and both have their pros and cons.

In fast drafting, your editing process can be much slower because your draft is far messier. However, in cycle drafting, your process of reaching The End is much slower, and it takes more time for you to unlock the "I wrote the first draft of a whole book" level of achievement.

The bigger drawback in cycle drafting is that if you decide to change something significant in the story, you have to go back and make substantial changes and sometimes delete entire sections of words you've not only already written but also polished. What's the point of spending any time editing words that you might decide not to keep? In fast drafting, you might make a bigger mess, but there's less wasted time, less wasted energy, and, in my opinion, a much deeper level of creativity engaged.

Editing as You Write

For new writers, editing as you write, sentence by sentence, word by word isn't a great idea. This process is why a lot of "aspiring authors" stay aspiring.

It takes *forever*. Every writer cuts stuff out before they finally finish, so you'll waste time and energy editing words that will never make the final novel. Also, in this method, there's no way to separate the creator from the editor.

Good novels are good stories. Get the story done first and then worry about the pretty sentences.

Later on, after you've written a few novels, perhaps this will be your method. If it gets the book written, then great, that's a successful process for you.

WRITING TOOLS

What are you actually going to use to write this first novel of yours?

Let's talk tools.

You don't need any special software or writing instruments to write a book. Still, some things make the process easier to organize, and if you're like most writers I know, having dedicated Writer Things is simply nice. All you really need is something to write your story in and something to capture your notes with.

Word Processing Software

Scrivener

Scrivener is a word processing software designed especially for writers. It helps organize long-form writing projects with ease and provides space to keep all of your notes alongside your actual work. It comes with a variety of templates, including one for novels.

Many complain Scrivener is too hard to use because it takes too long to learn all the features. Yes, there are heaps of features, but Scrivener is only as complicated as you need it to be. I've been using Scrivener for about fifteen years and have only just scratched the surface on all of its capabilities. There's no need to learn everything before you start—simply choose a blank template and start writing, picking up what you need to know as you need to know it. There are different books and courses available to help you learn to harness the power of this tool.

At the time of writing, Scrivener is available for Mac, iOS, and Windows. Late in 2019, the developers announced they were working on a new Android version, but as of early 2024, this is yet to be released and maybe never will be.

Scrivener isn't free, but it's also not terribly expensive, so if buying a license is within your means, I urge you to consider it. Writing a novel is hard enough, so why not use a dedicated software designed to make it easier?

Why Can't You Just Use MS Word or Google Docs?

You absolutely can, and many do. But…

The problem with these traditional word processors is that they have a linear view. You need to scroll through hundreds of pages when you want to backtrack into your book. With Scrivener, all of your chapters and scenes, however you choose to divide your work, are displayed right beside your drafting screen so you can jump around easily, change the order of things, and always see, just at a glance, where you're up to. There's also a corkboard feature if index cards are your thing, and you can even color-code sections. Who doesn't like color coding?

Ywriter

If you're unable to or not sure you want to invest in Scrivener, YWriter is a similar program (though far more basic). At the time of writing, it's completely free. Ywriter was developed by Australian author, Simon Haynes, so you know a program designed by an author is always going to best serve an author's needs.

Note Software

I also recommend a handy note-taking program. Even if you don't write down every idea as it comes along, a note-taking system on hand lets you capture things like opening lines or snips of perfect dialogue. These things tend to appear in your brain when you're away from the writing desk, so carrying around a capturing tool is a good idea.

A small notebook in the handbag or pocket works well, but I've come to use digital note systems more and more (though I still own several billion notebooks and carry one in my handbag).

OneNote is a sophisticated note-taking and organizing app from Microsoft. It has full functionality for free, or it comes as part of the Microsoft 365 paid package.

OneNote syncs nicely across all platforms and devices. Its user-friendly interface of notebooks and pages makes keeping notes for multiple projects simple. I have even used this file structure system to outline books. It's good for collecting links, images, text, audio, video, and drawings (if your device has drawing capability).

OneNote has a nifty quick note shortcut feature, something I often use, particularly for those lightning strike moments.

I previously used EverNote, which is also great; however, the developers limited the basic free version to two devices. OneNote proved a perfect alternative that, for my needs and the needs of most novelists, does precisely the same thing as EverNote.

Grammarly and ProWritingAid

Grammarly and ProWritingAid are spelling, grammar and style checking apps. Any native spell-checker only goes so far. After that, there are these beasts.

Both systems detect less obvious typos, repeated words, frequently mixed-up words, punctuation gaffes, sentence structure issues, passive voice, and oodles more. The free version of Grammarly is limited but workable. The pro version checks for a greater variety of potential errors and also comes as an MS Word and Google Docs add-in and extensions for various browsers. On the desktop and web version, Grammarly has a limit to how many words it checks in one go, so you need to paste your writing in chunks.

ProWritingAid is very similar but has the added functionality of working directly in Scrivener and working with very long content—like a full novel—in the desktop apps.

For novels, I don't use this checking software until I'm sure I've written everything the way I want it. It's that stage that we'll be covering in the next module on Editing and Revision.

Generative AI Tools

At the time of writing this book, generative AI tools like ChatGPT and Sudowrite have only recently come into general public attention. Even with such a recent emergence, the writing world is abuzz with talk about these tools and the fact they can theoretically output a novel in about the same time as it takes most of us to write a scene.

We've already talked a little about how AI tools are capable of generating basic commercial genre novels to a decent, market standard. This isn't a book about how to write a novel with AI, how to compete in an AI saturated market, or the ethics of generative AI (though these are all critical topics in the AI conversation).

At the time of writing, in my experience, AI can't write a whole novel without substantial editing from a human. Sure, this way of engineering a novel is faster than actually writing one, but we're not quite at the stage of the bots being able to spit out a full novel on their own. There's no doubt in my mind that the technology will advance and the day that AI can write a book all by itself will be here before we know it. But I'm still not scared of that, and neither should you be. AI might be taking over many jobs in many industries, but there will always be human writers and artists.

Even when the tech advances to complete instant novel capabilities, I want to assure writers that AI tools can be used as a powerful writing aid without letting the robots write our stories.

AI can be a valuable and fun ideation tool, presenting us with ideas we might never have before considered. AI an also be useful for revising marketing copy like book blurbs and advertising content, but in these early stages of writing your first novels, you're probably not there yet.

There are a long list of moral and legal considerations around using AI to generate even basic content, let alone entire novels. And rightly so. But this shouldn't force authors away from experimenting with these tools as valuable helpers in the writing journey. At present, I use ChatGPT and Sudowrite, as well as image generating software like Midjourney, to help me generate ideas. I think of them as brainstorming assistants, and find them a whole lot of inspirational fun. I take my own ideas, feed them to the bots, and see what results. Then, I take these ideas, develop and meld them further. Sometimes these AI provided ideas are nonsense, ridiculous, or just don't fit. Other times these ideas are gold.

These tools aren't going anywhere. In fact, they're coming more and more, and will soon be integrated into our everyday tech even more than they already are (remember, predictive text is basic generative AI). Even if you choose not to use these tools, it's important to understand how they are being used in our industry, what they are capable of, and how your books might sit alongside AI books in an increasingly saturated market.

CHAPTER SUMMARY

Remember, there are as many ways to write a novel as there are novels in the world. While your process does develop as you write, start by choosing one way and see how it works for you. Also, please don't waste your time playing with the tools of the trade, learning their ins and outs before you write. Start writing and adapt as you move through the process.

In Summary...

- Plotting is outlining the story, or at least the main points of the story before you start writing.
- Discovery writing, also known as Pantsing, is making the whole thing up as you go along.
- You can both outline and discovery write in the same manuscript, different books, or however works best for you. It's a spectrum.
- Fast drafting means writing the whole first draft (or Alpha draft), beginning to end, and not stopping to fix a thing—a most empowering way to write.
- Cycle drafting is fast drafting a small amount, going back and editing before continuing to the next scene.
- Dedicated writing tools make the novel writing process more manageable, but are not mandatory.
- Generative AI is a present day reality of the writing industry that all writers should at least be aware of how to use and how to create a writing career alongside.

After you reach the end of your first draft, no matter the process or tools you used to get it done, it's going to need revising before it's ready for the world. Now, let's talk about editing.

CHAPTER 7
THE EDITING PROCESS

The End.

For me, typing those final two words into the Alpha draft, no matter how crappy a mess I've made of the previous 70,000ish words, it's a moment of pure elation. It's relief, it's pride, it's satisfaction and happiness. It's also not the end of the work.

After a suitable break time to rest your frazzled synapses after all the effort of writing a massive story, it's time to turn that awfully messy Alpha draft manuscript into a real-life novel.

To do this, I have an eleven-stage editing process.

This revision process assumes you've written the first draft using the fast draft method, but even if you've cycle drafted, there'll be applicable information.

Each step involves going back to the start of your novel and working through the whole manuscript, start to finish, focusing on one thing at a time. When you finish that focus pass, go back to the beginning and start again with a different point of focus. This system is rather like a pyramid. You start at the bottom with the macro foundational stuff and move your way through to the micro until you're working on the individual words.

To be honest, the eleven-step process can take more than eleven steps. Exactly how many passes of your draft it takes will depend on how you're feeling about your story, and perhaps how much mess you made in your Alpha draft.

Some authors find printing out their work on actual paper better suits their editing mind. While it's lovely to hold the physical words on page in your hand, I find I prefer to save the trees and ink and edit digitally. Some authors find a middle ground in this by reading through their rough manuscript on their e-reader device to make it more like reading an actual book and make notes on paper as they read (some reading devices now have note taking features). Do what works best for your editing brain.

IN THIS CHAPTER...

- Finishing
- Big Picture Edits
- Revise For Setting and World-Building
- Revise For Scene Structure
- Revise For Character Action
- Revise For Elegant Prose
- Typos and Line Editing
- Final Checks For Word Choice and Flow
- Beta Readers and Professional Editors
- Revise With Reader / Editor Suggestions
- Final Proofreading

A Note Of Warning...

You will be tempted to edit micro things like words and sentence structures while in the macro passes. Do your time management a favor and only edit individual words and sentences once you're certain that section will survive until the final draft.

1 - FINISH IT

Is everything you want in your story there?

The story must be complete. It doesn't need to be fully cohesive, but it needs to be a sense of beginning, middle, and end.

The Alpha draft should also be about the length you'll want your final novel to be, but that's flexible. The first draft of my supernatural mystery novel, *A Maze of Murder*, ended at 35K. I then went back and wove in a subplot to link three books to a series, adding another 25-ish thousand words.

2 - BIG PICTURE EDITS – REVISING FOR STRUCTURE

Remember everything we talked about in chapters 4 and 5 regarding character arcs and narrative structure? This is where you make sure you've got it down.

Nope, we're still not worrying about micro corrections like typos at this point, but I do often correct anything that's sorely wrong (my words are often a victim of my frenzied freestyle typing method).

Go to the beginning and start reading. This is your macro editing pass.

What is your hook? What and where is your inciting incident?

Make sure your major plot points occur at the right time during the story. Remember, the inciting incident at the beginning, no later than 12%; the character accepting the mission and entering the story problem at about 25%; the plot turning midpoint at 50%; some kind of revelations at 25% and 75%.

Does your story make sense overall?

Does the character arc make sense? Is your character changing? Have you given them flaws and some motivating factor that haunts them? Do they realize something about themselves?

In this phase, I'll also make sure all characters generally act and react in the context of their personality, but we'll do a dedicated character action pass soon.

The Google Calendar Story Diary Method

When I'm writing my messy Alpha draft, I don't really think about in-story time. Characters do everything all at once; a week or more can pass in a few sentences. I'll fudge how long it takes someone to get from point A to point B. Characters go to bed eighteen times a night and have dinner three times a morning in weeks with nine days.

When I'm doing the first big structural draft, I take blank Google Calendar—it doesn't matter which year or month—and add in a Story Diary. Character A does something, mark it down according to the time of day. What are they doing in the next scene? Where are they? What time is it? How much time needs to have taken place? What are the other characters doing? Mark it all down in the appropriate days and weeks. This is especially handy when writing simultaneous timelines with multiple protagonists.

When writing in my *Witch Against Wicked* world, I also used these calendars to track the moon phases for werewolf shifting purposes, so I don't end up with three full moons a month. For that same series, I used a yearly calendar to track the time between multiple books and make sure the seasons line up.

3 - REVISE FOR SETTING AND WORLD-BUILDING

In this step, we're looking at your story location.

Where is everything happening? How are the characters interacting with their environments?

Is everything happening where it should be happening? Is everyone in the right place?

Have you described your setting appropriately?

If your story takes place in a real-life location, this is the point where you would be doing any additional research and adding in any details you need to really bring your story to life. Remember, even made-up places require real-world reality, so now check how credible your world-building is.

4 - REVISE FOR SCENE STRUCTURE

Remember, a scene structure is like an entire novel. It starts with an inciting incident, and it moves through to a midpoint shift. Complications happen, and then everything culminates in action or revelation. Remember Conflict, Choice, Consequence.

Something needs to happen in every scene. Every scene needs to drive the whole story along through the flow of consequences. Now's the time to make sure that happens. Any scene that doesn't change and move the story forward gets completely revised or thrown to the cutting room floor.

During the scene-level pass, I'll also ensure my themes are strong and referenced in every chapter. I'll also be checking to make sure that any tiny detail foreshadowing I need is in place. Do you want to give your readers a hint of what's coming? Want to show how that vase Granny conveniently uses as a weapon in the final scene got into the kitchen? Weave it into the earlier scenes now.

5 - REVISE FOR CHARACTER ACTION

I'm talking here about the little physical actions that weave through scenes. What are people doing as they're talking, thinking, etc.? I've heard this referred to as the Visceral Pass as it shows in a more physical sense what characters are going through.

In my Alpha drafts, most of my characters nod and smile, sometimes grimace, every single time they speak. There's also a lot of staring and shrugging.

In this pass, make sure they're moving and acting like human beings. Give them little tasks to do, let them physically interact with others and their environment, make sure their physical reactions reflect what's happening in the scene.

A highly recommended resource for this stage is *The Emotion Thesaurus* by Angela Ackerman and Becca Puglisi. It's an index where you look up the emotion you're seeking to portray and then select an internal or external sensation or action from the extensive lists.

This is also the time to make sure that your characters are speaking distinctly. Many authors, even established novelists, write early drafts with every character speaking in the same style. We call it "monomouth." In real life, everyone speaks differently, so make sure this comes across in your book. An excellent way to do this is to make sure you can tell who is talking just from the dialogue without any "she/he/they said" attribution tags.

6 - REVISE FOR ELEGANT PROSE

By now, your manuscript essentially has everything it needs. Next, we turn to making the smaller components work. Here we look at paragraphs, making sure the right scene emphasis happens at the right paragraph points and also sentence structure.

I'm a fan of short, choppy sentences, but too many together makes for terrible reading, so I'll make sure there's a balance of long flowing sentences with quick impact statements. Reading your work out loud helps at this point.

As I'm editing for these small details, I'll also be keeping an eye out for anything I might have missed in the last passes.

Most authors at this stage will also be working on cutting words.

What? Like, delete parts from my story? Seriously?

Yes. Seriously.

Most of us write too much. We repeat the same points,

give unnecessary details, or write bits and pieces that do nothing to serve our stories.

This is the phase to tighten up all your scenes, paragraphs, and sentences to ensure every word is working in your favor. General guidelines suggest cutting ten percent of the total number of words, but this is highly variable.

7 - TYPOS AND LINE EDITING

I don't bother with the spell-check during the Alpha drafting, and I suggest, if you can stand it, you do the same. Through all of these passes, I have been getting rid of the wiggly red lines. Yet a few always remain by this step, so this is where I get the rest. I'll also be on the lookout for those words like homonyms or AutoCorrect replacements that basic spell check doesn't find. I'll run the whole thing through ProWritingAid at this point and then move the manuscript from Scrivener into Word or Pages, ready to format for my editor.

8 - FINAL CHECKS FOR WORD CHOICE AND FLOW

At this stage, you'll essentially have a finished novel. But there's always something. Keep reading until you think there's nothing left to change.

Once you're happy, go and work on something else for a week or two. I find writing nonfiction here is an excellent palate cleanser, or I'll often write a short story or something entirely different from the novel.

When I return to the novel, editing at this point is usually minor, from Step 5 of this structure onward.

At this point, I like to read the whole book aloud at least once. Another useful trick here is to use the text-to-voice function on your computer to read it back to you. This AI voice is a great teacher. Since it reads without perfect human inflection, it's an excellent way to examine the book word by word as you read along with the computer voice.

Reading out loud is how you find the flow of sentences. I don't like to repeat words too close to one another or have too many similar-sounding words in one sentence unless it's for a particular effect. Tip: Make sure your character names are all very different. A Tom and a Tony or an Adele and an Adie together are going to confuse readers.

This word variation is especially important if you're thinking of ever recording an audiobook version of your story. Whoa! Publishing an audiobook a little beyond the writing your first novel stage, but it's always good to prepare for these potential career developments at the ground level. As you read, pretend you're performing for an audiobook or live reading at your novel launch. It not only helps to fine-tune your prose, it's also fun!

9 - FIRST READERS AND PROFESSIONAL EDITORS

Now the book is ready for other eyes. And I don't mean publishing… yet. I don't always use beta readers or critique partners, but when I do, this is where I send it out to them. More on beta readers and critique partners in the next chapter.

I do always employ an editor. When I think my book is the best I can make, I'll have my editor do an in-depth edit along with the usual line edit and proofread.

If you're going indie, working with an editor is non-negotiable.

If you're traditionally publishing, an editor here isn't mandatory, but an editor will get your manuscript in the best shape possible for prospective agents or publishers. We'll look at readers and types editors in the next chapter.

10 - REVISE WITH READER/EDITOR SUGGESTIONS

You don't need to accept anything an editor or beta reader suggests. It's your book, after all. But it's always worth considering their opinions and be clear on why you're choosing to reject or accept what they say.

Remember, you're all playing on the same side. These suggestions aren't personal attacks. Your editor and first readers are trying, just as you are, to make your story into the best novel it can be.

Happy with everything?

11 - FINAL PROOFREADING

It's always best to employ a second proofreader for the last check, but if you've already paid for an editor in Step 9, your economic reality might prevent this from happening.

If you can only afford one round of editing and have made corrections with more care and attention to detail than someone disarming a bomb, a beta reader might be able to help with a final proofread. If you can only do it yourself, read it aloud and have your computer read it to you again.

CHAPTER SUMMARY

This multi-stage process is highly effective and makes the task of shaping a rough draft into a finished novel so much more manageable than trying to fix everything at once.

In Summary…

- Finish the draft. Ensure you've got a beginning, middle, and end, no matter how rough.
- Macro edit for structure and overarching situations.
- Revise for setting.
- Revise for scene structure.
- Revise for physical character action and reaction.
- Revise for prose.
- Revise for typos and other micro errors (line editing).
- Seek out early reader's opinions if you so choose.
- Employ an editor.
- Revise with reader/editor opinions.
- Final proofreading.

If you thought it was good to have written The End on that Alpha draft, wait to see how incredible you feel when you've passed through all of these steps and come out at the end with an actual novel manuscript, ready for the public to read.

In the next chapter, we move the discussion to the world outside you and your story and examine what to do when you've finished your book. It's time for the Big P…

PUBLISHING.

CHAPTER 8
WHEN YOUR BOOK IS DONE

Why, in this book designed to help you start writing, have I included content about publishing?

It's easy to get so caught up in the idea of publishing and all the fame and fortune (or lack thereof) that follows that you forget about actually writing your book. While you're in the beginning phase, sure, your focus needs to remain on developing a workable writing habit and getting the book written, but thinking at least a little about the end game can help stave off the feeling that you're not getting anywhere.

Goals are valuable, even if the goal posts change shape and position along the way.

This next chapter is a bare-bones introduction to publishing options. It's not an in depth guide to how to publish a book, but rather an overview of options designed to start you thinking. The appendix contains a list of resources that delve deeper into the publishing world. But before we move onto that end goal stuff, I want to revisit mindset for a bit.

By the time you're truly ready to think about this chapter, you will have finished a book.

This. Is. Huge.

Celebrate.

The fabled statistic goes that something like 85% of people say they want to write a book, and only about 1% actually do it. Honestly, I have no idea where these numbers come from, but you hear it spouted out all the time… it must be true.

Whatever the statistics, writing a book is nothing short of astounding. We need to congratulate ourselves. At the end of that first draft, you have achieved BIG TIME! Forget celebrating when you sell or publish the thing, reward yourself at every milestone and shower yourself in love and adoration, and above all respect.

Take a rest.

Okay, now you're done with the party, and you're feeling rejuvenated, it's time to get back to work, and start moving to get the book published.

IN THIS CHAPTER…

- Beta Readers, Critique Partners, and Experts
- Professional Editors
- How To Publish A Novel

BETA READERS, CRITIQUE PARTNERS, AND EXPERTS

We talked a little about beta readers in the editing process, and now we get into depth about what a beta reader or critique partner does.

Many writers consider beta readers and critique partners invaluable and non-negotiable parts of the book writing process. I'm not one of those writers, and I'll get to why soon.

First, what do these terms actually mean?

Beta readers and critique partners are the first eyes on your unpublished manuscript that aren't your own (or a pro editor's).

The differences in these reading roles are subtle but important.

What's a Beta Reader?

A beta reader is your first reader. Their's is a value judgment. Some point out structural mistakes, typos, etc.; however, that kind of feedback isn't required from this kind of reader. A beta reader's job is to tell you if they liked your story or not, and if it made sense overall. If they don't want to finish reading it, ask them why and at what point they gave up. It's generally a good idea to get a beta reader who enjoys your type of books. There's little point asking in someone for their opinion on your hard sci-fi horror thriller if all they like to read is literary think pieces.

What's a Critique Partner?

A critique partner is like a beta reader, but their job is specifically looking for mistakes or problems and also pointing out what works well. The crit partner is more about the craft than whether the book is "liked" or not, but that can be a part of the critique process.

A critique partner is another writer. In contrast, a beta reader can be anyone even if they don't have any specific knowledge of writing craft.

Benefits of Beta Readers and Critique Partners

Your early readers can pick up any problems you've overlooked from the large structural issues, right down to typos, depending on what you ask from them.

There's a confidence benefit too. It's tough to share your work with others in the early stages, so having these formal relationships in place helps to get you used to showing your work to others.

Critiquing for other writers can also make you a better writer. If you're in a reciprocal critique arrangement, you get to exercise the part of your brain that finds and understands problems in stories, which means you'll get better at spotting them in your own work.

The Problems with Beta Readers and Critique Partners

I mentioned earlier that I'm not a writer who considers these helpers necessary. I believe there are many pitfalls new writers can fall into with these kinds of reading relationships.

Often, when we're starting, our writing connections are fellow amateur writers. And this is great. It's wonderful to connect with writers at all stages of the journey. However, if you're using a fellow amateur author for advice on more technical issues of craft, they may find problems that aren't there or don't matter, or they might give you completely wrong information.

For example, there's loads of so-called writing advice floating around in the universe that is taken out of context.

"Show, Don't Tell" is one of the most well known of these. Sometimes telling is entirely permissible, even preferred in a story. If you've got an amateur whose experience limits them from knowing this, they might prompt you to remove some perfectly good telling from your work and change it into some overblown showing sequence.

Further, you may get yourself an overzealous amateur critique partner eager to show off everything they've noticed that doesn't fit textbook writing advice. This can shatter your confidence, destroying your writing life before it has ever really taken you anywhere.

If you do choose to open your work up for feedback in these early stages, remember to consider a first reader's suggestions and opinions as just that—suggestions and opinions. You don't need to follow their recommendations if you don't want to. You'll get more confident in what makes a story work and your own writing voice as you write more.

Other Kinds of Early Readers – Experts and Sensitivity Readers

Depending on how you're feeling, you might decide that only certain parts of your work need help from a first reader —and only then for the content itself, not anything about the actual story mechanics. This is my approach.

For example, you might need a reader with particular expertise to fact check your work.

I have my Go-To Classics Guy—a fellow author who has considerable expertise in the field of Classics who advises me on Latin and Ancient Greek language (I write fantasy and I love a good bit of Latin in a spell), and mythological elements.

I've also spoken with police for advice on crime scenarios.

I am an Australian who typically writes in fictional US settings. I've never even been to the USA, and don't get me started on the differences between Australian and US English. I have a few American friends I regularly query about details (for example, is there an American equivalent to Australia's CWA?). My editor is also American and "Americanizes" my prose and picks up on other aspects of American culture that I overlook (for example, I didn't know until a few years ago that electric kettles aren't a common thing in the USA. I was astounded as every house in my experience has one). Sure, Google helps me out all the time, but often can't compare to direct help from humans.

Look around at the people in your life. What do they know? Ask in your Facebook groups, ask on Twitter. People are usually more than thrilled to talk about what they know, and you'll be surprised at how many experts you have in your life!

Depending on the type of book you've written, using a sensitivity reader can also be a good idea. A sensitivity reader is a beta reader employed to read for certain values in a work relating to complex issues like race, gender, disability, and other potentially triggering elements. A sensitivity reader with expertise in these areas ensures you are representing these situations fairly and accurately.

Besides these experts, I don't use beta readers or crit partners unless I'm genuinely unsure if something I've written works. I prefer to save that job for my professional editor.

PROFESSIONAL EDITORS

Do You Need to Hire a Professional Editor?

It depends.

If you're pursuing a traditional publishing deal with agents and a publishing house, hiring an editor is mostly optional. It can be a good idea to get your novel into the best shape possible before you try to sell it, but it's not compulsory.

If you're going the independent publishing route (also called self-publishing), then you need to employ a professional editor.

What Kind of Editor Do You Need?

There are different kinds of editors and different kinds of editing services.

A structural edit goes over the whole book looking at your narrative, character arcs, and making sure it's a well-functioning story.

At the other end of the spectrum, a proofreader makes sure your spelling and grammar are correct after a copyedit. The proofreader does not make editorial comments on the story structure or any other macro issues.

In the middle, there's line editing and copyediting. The level of detail an editor goes into here can vary by editor (as do the names they give these kinds of services), but it's essentially making sure everything makes sense and reads well without going into the bigger issues of story structure.

Some indie authors only hire copy editors. Some won't release without a structural edit. It's up to you and how much professional help you think you need, but while you're finding your feet, it's good practice to pay for a full structural edit at least for your first book so you are familiar with what a major edit will look for.

My editor provides me with a "Deluxe Copyedit." This is a highly detailed copyedit that checks for continuity between books in the series, fact accuracy, sentence structure, regional dialect, proofreading, and the like. If I'm unsure about anything more significant, I ask her to do a full structural edit.

And that brings us to the exciting end-stage of the book writing journey… publishing options.

HOW TO PUBLISH A NOVEL

We are fortunate enough to live in a time where writers have options. Lots and lots of options. This boils down to two general publishing paths: traditional publishing and independent publishing (self-publishing). Within each path there are a range of different options.

Traditional Publishing

Traditional publishing is where you hand your book over to a third party publishing house under a contract, and they pay you for it in either an advance or in royalties, or both. More often than not, these relationships will be organized for you through an agent. Some smaller publishers might not require you to work through an agent, but for the most part, going traditional will also mean signing to an agency.

Traditional publishing might mean going with one of the Big publishing houses. These used to be called the Big Five, but corporate mergers and restructuring happens all the time so this number changes.

Traditional publishing might also mean going with a small, independent publishing company. Even though it's an independent company, it's still traditional publishing as you're not publishing your own work.

Independent Publishing

Also called self-publishing or author publishing, indie authors publish and sell their own books. While I have had some short work published by traditional publishers, I am an independent author.

There are dozens of ways to publish and sell books as an indie author.

In the early days of indie publishing we used services like

Amazon's Kindle, Kobo, and Draft2Digital, and or print-on-demand services like IngramSpark.

These are still the most common indie author distribution options, but we now have other exciting paths in addition to these standard methods.

Online serial publishing is also an option with sites like Wattpad, Royal Road, Kindle Vella, Radish, and others.

Many authors are now using direct to reader sales models, selling their books from their own websites without having to give Amazon or the other retailers a cut of the sales.

Authors might also use subscription models to sell to their readers. This can be done through subscription service providers like Ream Stories, Patreon, or authors can set up their own unique systems via email list services.

Hybrid Publishing

Publishing doesn't need to be an either/or situation. An author can choose to self-publish some titles or seek tradi-tional publishing for other books. You can even pursue both for the same book, depending on which rights you retain. For example, if you sell your paperback rights to a traditional publisher, you might (depending on contracts) still be able to self-publish your ebook or audiobook or publish different formats in other parts of the world.

Before we get into the pros and cons of each publishing option, I want to get a *big* misconception out of the way first…

AUTHORS AND MARKETING

Many new (and not so new) authors say they will never consider indie publishing because they hate marketing themselves.

Sure, marketing can be awkward and uncomfortable and a lot of authors struggle here.

But, no matter which side of the publishing divide you choose, you will have to market yourself. In the traditional realms, you do get help with marketing—and you don't buy your own ads. Still, trad published authors have to show up to events, put themselves out there, develop an online platform, go on podcasts and panels, perhaps publish additional content solely for marketing purposes, and create a personal brand to sell books. In the indie publishing world, you do the same thing on your own steam (plus buy your own ads).

So please, when weighing up your options on which publishing path to go for, don't let the prospect of marketing influence your decisions in the wrong ways.

THE PROS AND CONS OF INDEPENDENT VS. TRADITIONAL PUBLISHING

Independent Publishing

Pros

- Full creative control
- No gatekeepers
- Complete ownership and control of your intellectual property
- Higher royalties
- Quick publishing turnaround
- Easy international publishing
- Many options for getting books to readers.

Cons

- More expensive outlay

- More work (formatting; advertising and marketing; hiring other professionals for cover design, editing, etc.; merchandise, etc.)
- Some traditional literary institutions still unrecognized (literary awards, membership groups, etc.), and there is a lingering stigma in some circles as "vanity publishing," which is rubbish but it's still a reality.

Traditional Publishing

Pros

- The publisher takes care of book layout, covers, editors, etc.
- Potential for high (but not necessarily higher) exposure, books in big retailers, etc., traditional advertising, etc.
- Possible positive psychological effect—you were "chosen" by the publishing gatekeepers.
- Some assistance with marketing.
- Access to some awards, competitions, memberships, etc.

Cons

- Little if any creative control over your final book product.
- Potential for limited global releases. Some books not published in all formats all over the world.
- Limited format releases. Some publishers might not give you an audiobook, or large print paperback, for example.

- Generally lower royalties than indie.
- Limited if any ownership or control over intellectual property.
- Slow process. It can take years to release once you sell a book.
- Many publishers also require you to have an agent to sell through.
- Complicated contracts.

The choice of which way to go is entirely yours. There's nothing setting your decision in stone either. Go in whichever direction suits you. If you change your mind, seek another path. You've worked hard. It's your book. You get to decide what happens to it.

CHAPTER SUMMARY

Many options in this chapter depend on what you want to happen to your book and how you want to publish it. Remember, you don't need to think about it in the early stages. Even if you decide how to publish before you finish, always put the writing first before using any time and energy looking for agents or researching how to self-publish.

In Summary…

- Beta readers and critique partners are optional but can be helpful.
- You can choose to pursue a traditional book deal or publish your book independently. Both sides have their pros and cons.
- Professional editors are necessary if you are independently publishing.
- Hybrid publishing means publishing in both traditional and self-published models. This can be for the same books depending on your traditional contracts.
- Every published author, regardless of their publishing model, needs to market themselves if they hope to sell books.

THE END.

That brings us to the end of our adventure in writing a book from idea to publication. I hope this information has inspired you, filled you with confidence and enthusiasm to stop saying "One Day" and finally, once and for all, start to write and, most importantly, finish that book you've always wanted to write.

You'll find a bunch of extra resources and notes in the appendix on everything we've covered in these chapters. We've gone into a lot, but this is just the tip of the iceberg.

That's what's so great about writing and publishing: there is always something new to learn, another perspective to consider, another way to do something, and another idea to blow your mind and create a fantastic book. And once you learn how to do it one way, a totally new way will come along to rock your writing world.

Whatever it looks like for you, I wish you all the success on your writing journey.

Write well, my friends.

Kate

RESOURCES AND FURTHER READING

MINDSET AND HABITS

- *The War of Art* - Stephen Pressfield
- *Daring Greatly* - Brene Brown
- *The Power of Vulnerability TED Talk* - Brené Brown.
- *Atomic Habits* - James Clear
- *Big Magic* - Elizabeth Gilbert
- *The Mental Game of Writing: How to Overcome Obstacles, Stay Creative and Productive, and Free Your Mind for Success* - James Scott Bell
- *The Successful Author Mindset* - Joanna Penn
- *Dear Writer, You Need to Quit* - Becca Syme

IDEAS AND STORIES

- *Steal Like an Artist* - Austen Kleon
- *Great Stories Don't Write Themselves* - Larry Brooks
- *Wonderbook* – James Vandermeer
- *Creativity* – John Cleese

THE MECHANICS OF STORY PART 1 - GENRE AND TROPES

- *TV Tropes* - www.tvtropes.org
- *Genre* - John Frow
- *Genre and Hollywood* - Steve Neal
- *A Semantic/Syntactic Approach to Film Genre* - Rick Altman. (Cinema Journal, Vol. 23, No. 3 (Spring, 1984), pp. 6-18)
- *The Anatomy of Genres* – John Truby

THE MECHANICS OF STORY PART 2 - CHARACTER ARCS

- *Creating Character Arcs* - K.M Weiland
- *Writer's Guide to Character Traits* - Dr. Linda N. Edelstein
- *The Mythic Guide to Characters* - Antonio del Drago
- *The Emotional Wound Thesaurus* - Angela Ackerman and Becca Pugulisi
- *13 Steps to Evil: How to Create Superbad Villains* - Sacha Black

THE MECHANICS OF STORY PART 3 - NARRATIVE STRUCTURE

- *The Three Story Method* - J Thorn and Zach Bohannon
- *Poetics* - Aristotle
- *The Hero of a Thousand Faces* - Joseph Campbell
- *The Virgin's Promise: A New Archetypal Structure* - Kim Hudson
- *The Story Grid* - Shawn Coyne
- *Save The Cat Writes A Novel* – Jessica Brody
- *Take Off Your Pants: Outline Your Books for Faster, Better, Writing* - Libbie Hawker
- *Story Engineering* - Larry Brooks
- *Structuring Your Novel: Essential Keys for Writing an Outstanding Story* - KM Weiland
- *The Anatomy of Story* - John Truby
- *Romancing the Beat* - Gwen Hayes
- Writing Excuses Podcast, Season 10 Episode 29 "Why Should My Characters Fail Spectacularly?"

PROCESSES AND TOOLS

- *Writing into the Dark* - Dean Wesley Smith
- *No Plot? No Problem* - Chris Baty
- NaNoWriMo - www.nanowrimo.org

- *2K to 10K: Writing Faster, Writing Better, and Writing More of What You Love* - Rachel Aaron
- *Bird by Bird* - Anne Lamott
- *The NaNoWriMo Survival Guide* – Kate Krake

THE EDITING PROCESS

- *Use the Power of Feedback to Write a Better Book* - Belinda Pollard
- *The Emotion Thesaurus* - Angela Ackerman and Becca Pugulisi
- *Write Great Fiction Revision And Self-Editing* - James Scott Bell

WHEN THE BOOK IS DONE

- *Marketing For Writers Who Hate Marketing* - James Scott Bell
- *Six Figure Authors Podcast* - Lindsay Buroker, Andrea Pearson, Jo Lallo (intermittent from 2023)
- *The Creative Penn Podcast* - Joanna Penn
- *The Self Publishing Podcast* - The Alliance of Independent Authors
- *The Pursuit of Perfection: And How it Harms Writers* - Kristine Kathryn Rusch
- *Wish I'd Known Then… For Writers Podcast* – Jami Albright and Sara Rosett
- *The Rebel Author Podcast* – Sacha Black

ABOUT THE AUTHOR

Kate Krake is the author of fantasy fiction, and personal and creative development for writers.

She is passionate about folklore, pop culture, long distance walking, and curious trivia. She can usually be found with her nose in a book, her ears in a song, and her head in the clouds.

Kate has lived all over Australia and currently lives in Perth, Australia, with her family.

Connect
www.katekrake.com
kate@katekrake.com

ALSO BY KATE KRAKE

FICTION

Night Shift At The Shadow Bay Hotel

Witch Against Wicked

A Maze of Murder

A Mask of Chaos

A Trial of Ghosts

A Wreath of Ruin

A Hex of Wolves

A Trick of Terror

A Coven of Demons

NONFICTION

The Creative Writing Life

Writing Beyond Fear

How To Be A Better Writer

The NaNoWriMo Survival Guide

How To Write Your First Novel

Tarot Writers

Tarot Spreads For Writers

One Word Tarot Meanings

Journal Arcana

Inkwell & Elm

www.inkwellandelm.com

Inkwell & Elm publishes premium resources to help writers and other creatives achieve success.

The Inkwell & Elm Group

The Creative Writing Life
www.thecreativewritinglife.com

Tarot Writers
www.tarotwriters.com

Writing Prompt World
www.writingpromptworld.com

www.ingramcontent.com/pod-product-compliance
Lightning Source LLC
Chambersburg PA
CBHW060044030426
42334CB00019B/2484